STAGE, SCREEN AND SANDWICHES

The Remarkable Life of Kenelm Foss

With all good wishes

Fanny Burney

STAGE, SCREEN AND SANDWICHES
The Remarkable Life of Kenelm Foss

Fanny Burney

ATHENA PRESS
LONDON

STAGE, SCREEN AND SANDWICHES
The Remarkable Life of Kenelm Foss
Copyright © Fanny Burney 2007

All Rights Reserved

No part of this book may be reproduced in any form
by photocopying or by any electronic or mechanical means,
including information storage or retrieval systems,
without permission in writing from both the copyright
owner and the publisher of this book.

ISBN 10-digit: 1 84401 908 X
ISBN 13-digit: 978 1 84401 908 3

First Published 2007 by
ATHENA PRESS
Queen's House, 2 Holly Road
Twickenham TW1 4EG
United Kingdom

Printed for Athena Press

*I dedicate this book to Bertie, my late husband,
to my son Brian, for all his help,
and to everyone who encouraged me,
which gave me the incentive to put pen to paper
and write this light-hearted tribute to my father.*

Foreword by Brian Woolnough

They say half the population doesn't eat properly, especially lunch. Eating on the go; a sandwich at your desk; coffee on the train, the carton balanced precariously as fellow passengers look at you over the top of their newspaper. Sometimes no lunch at all! A doctor regularly warns me to eat three balanced meals a day and to make sure there is always time to digest the food.

'When you get home in the evening,' he says, 'give yourself a period to relax before and after eating, and don't forget to exercise.' Is he mad? There isn't time for anything these days, apart from working. Life is a one-hundred-miles-an-hour chase and it appears to be going around in circles. It can't be good for us. The French seem to have it right. Whatever the circumstances, they stop for an hour and a half at lunchtime, to eat properly before returning to work feeling comfortable. For we English, it's indigestion and stress all the way. What are we doing to ourselves? It can't have always been like this, can it? The answer, it seems, is yes, it probably has been, and I can reveal that my family has to take some of the responsibility.

In 1925 a gentleman by the name of Kenelm Foss, my mother's father, and my grandfather, opened the first sandwich bar eat-in and take-away in the country, in Oxendon Street, Haymarket, London. He didn't know it then, but this extraordinary character, who achieved so much in his life in the theatre and film world, became the man to introduce what is now the fast food craze to England. His snack bars were called Sandy's, a chain that became a phenomenal success. Charlie Chaplin, Noel Coward, George Bernard Shaw, Rex Harrison, Edgar Wallace and Prime Minister Ramsay MacDonald were all friends and regular visitors. If you were anyone you were spotted at Sandy's. In his autobiography, Harrison wrote: 'Sandy's was definitely the place to be seen in!'

Kenelm Foss was Sandy. His takeouts were the McDonald's

and Pret à Manger of his day. What these companies provide for the public and stand for in 2006 stemmed from the idea of a man who realised that after the First World War the people needed something different. They were fed up with dressing up and waiting in long queues at restaurants, anticipating change in their lives; he gave them instantly healthy fresh food.

His slogans were simple: 'Where and what is Sandy's?' and 'Fast food, no waiting'. His wife, children and friends helped him run it, having been told, 'There is only one way to give the public fresh sandwiches – make them ourselves.' And they did. All day, every day. The demand was so great – success so instant – the Haymarket store opposite Sandy's delivered cut bread eight times daily. The public took to this new idea with excitement and raw enthusiasm, and to get inside Sandy's meant waiting with other Londoners, the line often stretching up and around the neighbouring Prince of Wales Theatre. The first day was so congested that police had to be called to control the crowd!

The fillings were all Foss's idea. How about kedgeree, a mixture of haddock and egg, laced with his own chutney sauce? The Indian cricketer, Prince Duleepsinhji, loved them so much that he once ate fourteen rounds in one visit! Partridge, pheasant, grouse or wild duck were also favourites. Nut butter, lemon curd, farmer's relish, home-made Scottish fish paste, hard or soft roes, plus all the obvious standards, sold every day. My grandmother, Elizabeth, led the team making them downstairs, often cursing at the demand.

There were an unbelievable 150 varieties to choose from. Sixty promised each day and the take-out service was free and guaranteed within a certain time. On the menu, which was the actual size of the sandwich, was printed, 'Shellfish, no tinned food, no foreign produce, no tips and no waiting.' The average price was six old pennies and the number to call 'Central 5954'. Wonderful stuff. Sandy's was a massive success.

He had favourite stories, of course, and warmly told this one of the then-King, Edward VII, who was a huge fan of Sandy's. The sandwich he liked most of all was a certain cheese variety, a filling the King's personal chef put my grandfather on to. The filling had to be between brown bread without butter, consisting of fifty per cent grated cheese, preferably Stilton, ripe but dry, thirty per cent finely chopped celery; then a hint of parsley. Woe betide him if there was not a supply ready for the King at his shooting parties or visits to the races.

I loved this note inside his menus: 'Ladies may enter alone with the utmost assurance of courtesy and consideration in every way and from all who may be present.'

He decided to expand, and the next Sandy's – perhaps the most popular and successful – arrived at 65 Fleet Street, on the corner of Bouverie Street. How ironic that I should spend so many of my early days on national newspapers walking past that very spot. The *Sun* newspaper, which I joined in 1973, had its offices in Bouverie Street before moving to Wapping. With colleagues, lunchtime was a glass of wine or two, a sandwich or coffee somewhere along my favourite street in London. In those days in the early seventies it remained in the heart of the newspaper industry. You could smell the stories and the characters; hear them if you stayed long enough in the pubs.

There was always someone who wanted to reminisce. It is with regret now that I look back and wish I had spent more time studying a family history that had developed literally before my eyes. Pubs around the *Sun* building in the early seventies still had sawdust on the floor. Those were the days when journalists interviewed contacts over their pints instead of having to be in the office; when there were no mobile phones; when you sensed the history. Sandy's had been at the heartbeat of that. 'Journalists need sustenance,' said Kenelm Foss. 'We'll open in Fleet Street twenty-four hours a day.'

His staff of eleven quickly rose to forty to meet the demand. Elizabeth, my grandmother, used to trudge home at midnight, a few sandwiches and the day's takings in her handbag. A feature of the sandwich bars was the wooden wall panelling, decorated by national artists with portraits of the famous – many of them signed – while stars like Chaplin autographed pound notes and stuck them on the walls.

Regular customers included revue girls and well-known actors and actresses, artists; famous faces mixing with the public. Three sides of a room were all autographed by the famous, like Gertrude

Lawrence, Beatrice Lillie, Sybil Thorndike and Fay Compton. It was a roaring success in the roaring twenties. The *Weekly Dispatch* described it like this:

> Women in gorgeous lamé cloaks sit on high stools and rest their feathered fans upon the bar counter, while their escorts sit holding their silk hats, waiting for the sandwich of their choice.

The New York *Herald Tribune* paid special tribute to Mr Foss's 'little joint'. I particularly liked his first day Fleet Street menu in honour of the stars, a series of special sandwich titles. There were choices such as Custard Pie, in honour of Charlie Chaplin, with an ingredient of lemon curd; Film Fan for Ivor Novello, made with banana and cream; or The Vegetarian for Bernard Shaw with 'the ingredient' that you never could tell.

Where are all those signatures and panels today? How my mother would love to know. Her father left everything to her in his will, but great items of value went missing. She is left with hundreds of cuttings, photographs, scrapbooks, letters and, of course, most importantly of all, her memories. You can't buy those and this is the story of her father by her – the first book she has written, and painstakingly scribbled in longhand at the age of eighty-five! Would she have liked to have written it before? Yes, of course. Why didn't she? It's impossible to answer, other than to say that you have to go when the inspiration and feeling is right.

Now I know more, I would have liked to have spent time in my grandfather's company, asking him about those days when Charlie Chaplin sat in his snack bar, eating his sandwiches, sipping his coffee (the best in London by the way), gossiping; when deals were done, contracts signed. Foss went from making films to making sandwiches and all the time made friends. At the age of five, I had no idea what he had achieved in his life, what he stood for or the stories he had to tell. He died in 1963 at the age of seventy-eight and it was an opportunity missed by me, someone who loves stories and the history of the great actors and actresses of days gone by. I can't beat myself up over it, and I am happy to learn more and write this foreword from this distance.

He was a man of many talents, an impatient man, often over-ambitious, and someone who lost interest too easily. He had thought of the idea of a sandwich bar after visits to America and Scotland and rose to the challenge of a friend who simply said to him: 'You keep talking about a sandwich bar – why don't you do it then?' He did and then allowed the dream to carry him too far.

Kenelm kept opening new bars; one in Brighton where the manager he left in control fleeced him, and the overheads became too much. There was competition from others as people realised that fast food was a market to develop. He suddenly found himself surrounded by competition and yet, instead of keeping just success with one or two Sandy's, he opened new bar after new bar and eventually had to close down. It seems wrong to dismiss the end of what was a phenomenon so easily, but that basically is how it was. The men who had backed him at the start wanted their money back and he closed Sandy's with hardly a profit to show. The rich and the famous went off somewhere else. That's life; there is always something new, someone else. Keeping up, maintaining levels and success is the secret of the business.

How Kenelm Foss badly needed guidance or an agent to push him in the right direction. He was a man with so many good ideas and should have made a fortune. He didn't. He once told my mother how Vera Lynn was a friend and how he wished he had asked to be her manager; he would have made a fortune. He never once put a patent on any of his ideas and never protected his life in the theatre and film world. He was a romantic who loved life and never worried about the future. Many will relate to that. Sandy's was his greatest and most famous achievement, but there were hundreds of plays he wrote and produced, plays and films he acted in, poems he wrote and film sets he designed. Once, when running The Little Theatre in the Strand, London, he persuaded the famous playwright, G K Chesterton, to write a play for him. It was called *Magic* and another outstanding success was born.

His mind ticked all day every day, full of ideas. After Sandy's he went off in a different direction. In London the public went *to* his fast food bars, so this time he decided to take the food to them. Those who lived in the country and who could not travel to London would be served on their doorstep. Enter the first Fish and Chip takeaway service. Kenelm Foss invented the phrase

'Chish and Fipps' – again no patent for financial reward – and once more there was success.

This is the story of his life through the eyes of my mother, Fanny Burney, who is a distant relation of the famous authoress of the same name. In many ways it is a tragic story, with the death of two of his children and his own suffering with TB, a story punctuated with highs and lows, of a man who gave pleasure to so many people and who constantly asked questions of himself. It is difficult to describe him because he did so much. How can we relate today to the King of England mixing with famous and rich, the public and the poor, in a café in London, demanding his favourite sandwiches? Foss was often called the Sandwich King, but he was much more than that.

Yet when you next pop into a fast food store and order a take-out sandwich or coffee, spare a thought for the man who began it all: Kenelm Foss, my grandfather, who one day had an idea and saw it rocket. He will have had no idea that at the turn of the century fast food would be so massive across the world. Lunch has never been the same since Sandy's.

We all have dreams and he, more than most, made them come true. The fact that he died with nothing to show for it, apart from the scrapbooks, cuttings and memories my mother owns and constantly pores over, is just part of the story. A roller-coaster ride of stage, screen and sandwiches. I'll let my mother tell it in her own unique way, from an era that I can only read about and wonder.

Brian Woolnough, 2005

Chief Sports Writer with the *Daily Star* newspaper, former football correspondent and associate sports editor of the *Sun*, Sky Television presenter currently co-hosting *Sunday Morning Supplement* with Jimmy Hill, radio presenter and regular contributor to *Radio 5 Live* and writer of fourteen books on football.

Preface

How, When and Why I Decided to Write this Book

I guess the best way to write a book is to start at the very beginning, go on writing until you come to the very end, and then stop.

This is what I propose to do here… and the very beginnings of this book are in the year 1885 with the birth of my father, Kenelm Foss.

I don't think the fact that during his busy life he became an author, with fifteen published books to his credit, will make it any easier for me to write my own book.

When my father died in 1963, he left me all his diaries, scrapbooks and newspaper cuttings. Ever since, he and his magical life have been on my mind, more or less. There had been talks of a documentary about him, but nothing came of it.

I wrote around to numerous influential people for help, including Dylis Powell, but no joy. So, a little deflated, I gave up for a while, often thinking of other ways and always hoping, but to no avail.

One of the reasons, I think, was the fact that, although the diaries and scrapbooks were mine, I did not actually receive them until my stepmother died, almost twenty years after my father. I understand she was approached regarding the documentary, but for some reason was not interested. Why? We don't know; maybe she was not bothered, we will never know!

Then, as so often happens in life, albeit many years later, things suddenly became clear to me. In 2002, while watching *Eastenders* on the television, a new character emerged. Wham! He was called Alfie Moon and hundreds of thousands of watching female admirers (of all ages more or less) fell under his spell. Shane Richie was the actor who played him with such charm. Eyes were glued to the screen whenever he was on.

Shane was an instant success, as everyone knows. Even my

little great-grandson Joe, aged three at the time, would come into my room, hold his arms out wide and say, 'Alfie Moon!' Shane then wrote a book, his autobiography called *Rags to Richie*, which came out in November 2003. That was it! The exact time of my eighty-fifth birthday and I asked my family to buy it as a present for me. At my birthday tea I picked the book up and said with a laugh, 'If I ever write a book about my father, I will call it *From Riches to Rags*.' (For that is pretty well true!) A short while afterwards, I realised it was also one hundred years to the day, near enough, that my father had first taken to the stage!

My granddaughter Emma said, 'Well, why don't you write a book?'

'Me, write a book? Not in a million years!' Then, later on that day, I said to myself, *Well, OK, why not? Yes, I will have a go*. So out I went and bought a large A4 pad, took my pen in my hand and, as it touched the paper, it just flowed and I could not stop writing for over six months. Even now I think of more information to add to the story; I loved doing it.

I did it for my father because he deserved it and I hope he approves. So you see, Shane was, indirectly, the very reason I started writing the book. It was the incentive I needed and I thank him from the bottom of my heart, and for Alfie, a lovely character – we shall all miss him!

I didn't blame anyone when I found many important papers about my father were missing from the will; they were probably sold when money was tight. The thing I would have liked most were many of the letters written to my father by all the famous people of that era. And now I know where they are! We found them on the Internet; but it is too late. Oh well! Such is life.

Another fascinating thing that occurred later on was also unbelievable, sort of a dream. Some friends and relatives had told me about a wonderful lady medium, Dorothy Chitty. A few of the family had visited her and were amazed by what she told them. I felt I would like to see her, so I arranged a visit. My daughter-in-law drove me up to Ealing, where we met. When my turn came, I sat there with my hands in my lap wondering what was coming next. It was nothing like I thought it was going to be, but I was still a little nervous. She talked about numerous things and people from my past and then suddenly became very excited.

'I see writing,' she said. 'Lots of it, pages of it, page after page. A book maybe! Are you writing a book by any chance?'

I was now smiling, I couldn't believe what I was hearing. She looked at me and asked, 'Well, are you?'

'Yes,' I said. 'I was wondering if you were going to mention it.'

'Oh, yes,' Dorothy said. 'Well it is going to be published very soon!'

I was elated, such a wonderful feeling. As we left, I said to her, 'If my book is ever published, I will let you know and send you a copy.'

'If?' she said. 'It *is* going to be published and that is a fact!'

With the medium's words still in my mind and a reborn enthusiasm for both myself and my father's illustrious career, a most amazing coincidence happened whilst on a trip to see a show in London. I was with my daughter and granddaughter in 2001; our taxi driver took an unexpected shortcut through Oxendon Street, so I instinctively turned my head to see what the Sandy's building looked like after such a long time! It was sixty years since I was last there! 'Oh no!' I said. 'It is a *unisex hairdresser's*! But that's life I suppose!'

And what were we going to see at the Prince of Wales Theatre? Why, *Fosse* of course! What else?

Kenelm Foss, aged seventeen

In the Early Days

My grandfather was very fond of Ken (my father). Every morning, weather permitting and when he was old enough, Ken would accompany him to the station before he left for London each day, hand in hand and helping him with his heavy bag, amusingly referred to as 'the sack'! This was a sort of ritual, but thoroughly enjoyed by both. The family lived in a large house in Croydon, Surrey, my grandfather being an eminent solicitor and three times Mayor of Croydon, who worked in London in Fenchurch Street and was always seemingly busy. My father's mother is remembered as rather cold, stern and uncaring. He supposed that having so many children (eleven in all) had become rather tedious and monotonous – but they did have a wonderful nanny/nurse who lived in and was always there for them whenever they needed her, with a large comforting bosom to cry on whenever things went wrong. In short, she was a lady, and, in the opinion of Kenelm's first wife, the only woman Kenelm ever really loved. Her name was 'Harvey' and she made all their lives happy whenever they were home, which wasn't very often, as the boys (six brothers) were sent to public schools at an early age – all of them going to, and boarding at, different ones for some reason.

Eastbourne having proved beneficial to my father's weak chest it was decided that he should follow his brother Ted to the Abbey School, Beckenham. At that time it was an absolutely model private school, in appearance and in every other way. The entrance gates, the long drive through the playing fields, with glimpses of fives, racquet-courts, gym, swimming baths, sanatorium, and under-masters' house... and the really thrilling quadrangle, girt about with cloisters, creeper-covered buildings and cobble-paved archway, with surmounting shield and motto: FUNGOR OFFICIUM COTIS ('I perform the office of a whetstone').

Kenelm had nothing but pleasant recollections of the Abbey School, where his particular friend was Ben Travers, the writer of those record-breaking Aldwych Theatre farces, *A Cuckoo in the Nest*, *Thark*, etc. Ben was always on the small side, and Ken the opposite, so they were 'the long and the short of it' to all the school. In footer-shorts Ken's bare knee used to be about four times the size of Ben's.

They were both, even then, stage-struck; and together they organised a not-officially-recognised School Dramatic Society. They sent for lists of one-act plays from French's, made a selection, and rehearsed assiduously. One piece they did was called 'Doctor Diaculum', and in it Ken had to wear a long white beard on wire, looped over the ears. Their stage was the raised dais in Big School used by officiating clergy at divine service, and the price of admission was two ginger biscuits or garibaldis ('squashed flies') for the first two rows or pews, two Petit-Beurre or Nice biscuits for the next two, a single ginger for the next few, and so on down the scale.

In any case they were a huge success, and there was not a word of truth in the subsequent allegation by that professional humorist, Ben Travers, that Ken had scoffed the whole of the takings, causing a strike on Ben's part that bust up the project. He rather lost sight of Kenelm for a while after that. Then years later, he encountered him one day in London, just outside the Garrick Theatre. Ken was then somewhere in his early twenties I suppose. His appearance took Ben's breath away. He had adopted to the uttermost limit the almost defiant costume, gait and general demeanour of the old bohemian Victorian actor of tradition. He was at that time playing a very subsidiary part in *The Exploits of Brigadier Gerard* by Conan Doyle, in which Lewis Waller appeared as actor-manager. Of course Ben went to see it.

After attending the Abbey School, my father was sent to Malvern and then to Wellesley's school of art, for my grandfather would have dearly liked him to become an artist. He was exceedingly clever at all forms of art: oils, watercolours, sketching, etc., but fate stepped in. My father's sisters all did well for themselves, considering they were all only taught at home by tutors, with four of them becoming headmistresses (teachers) in schools around the world, including one in Malta and two in George, South

Africa! My aunt, Josephine Foss MBE, became the most celebrated of all as she founded the Pudu English School for girls in Malaya in the late twenties; but more of her trials and tribulations in life later…

In his teens, my father and his friends were all mad about the theatre, and they put on many amateur shows in halls around Croydon. His greatest friends were the Pertuis brothers and Lewis Casson who, although somewhat older than he, were wonderfully suited and remained friends for the rest of their lives. They all shared digs together later on; Lewis became a very well-known actor, Roland Pertuis a writer, and one of Roland's sons, Jon Pertwee, found fame playing Doctor Who and Worzel Gummidge. (The Pertuis family changed the spelling of their surname to Pertwee, to avoid confusion of the pronunciation.) Roland's other son became a commander in the Royal Navy and, by an amazing coincidence, my son-in-law served on the same ship, HMS *Yarmouth*.

My father, meanwhile, had made up his mind that he wanted to make the stage his career and as luck would have it he got the chance from a cousin, George R Foss, a well-known actor/manager who got him a walk on part at a London Theatre, The Court, run by Granville Barker, a celebrated stage manager of that time, who took Dad under his wing.

Early Theatre Days

My father shared an apartment with Lewis Casson at the beginning of his career. It was in Clifford's Inn, London. My father, Kenelm Foss, had been touring with the Lewis Waller Company, as actor and understudy in the English provinces. When he returned to London it was Henry Ainley who carted Ken along to the Drury Lane Theatre, to understudy Ainley and to play the part of a brutal warder in Hall Caine's *The Bondman*. Mrs Patric Campbell was the leading lady, though anyone less suitable for that 'autumn drama' galere is unthinkable.

Lewis Casson was still with Vedrenne-Barker at The Court theatre; this was the period of the first ever stagings of *Major Barbara* and *Captain Brassbound's Conversion*.

Though Lewis Casson and Kenelm Foss had been closely associated for the previous year or two, it was not until Ken went to Drury Lane that they set up house together, and then probably only because Ken's engagement there guaranteed him ten weeks certain at £6 a week, in addition to his father's £1 a week allowance.

They were entirely as one in selecting Clifford's Inn as their abode; indeed, they agreed on most other subjects. Ken had heard folk express surprise, amongst them Dame Sybil's versatile brother, Russell Thorndike, that two such very different types of men as Lewis and Kenelm could ever have been such intimate friends; but in explanation Ken would invariably say that his Lewis was not the Sir Lewis of popular belief, i.e. an uneasy amalgam of rebel crank and magisterial Chairman of Committees, less of an actor than a shrewd Welsh impresario, whose wife largely owed her Sarah-Siddons-like eminence to his deft manipulation.

Kenelm thought of him, first and last, as an enthusiast of all the arts, a discriminating critic of them (save, perhaps of his own acting), quite unaffected, a mid-highbrow, a sahib, a perfectly straight man, a kind one, a sincere one – even when obstinately bigoted – with a sense of fun, and totally indifferent to appearances. Neither a money-grubber nor a swanker. In short, a very good type of Bohemian, despite an underlying conventionalism, churchgoer-cum-paterfamilias, which wasn't really *him* at all, but a throwback to the stock from which he sprang. The two of them had a delightful flat at the top floor of No. 16 Clifford's Inn. Passing, at the open entrance door in the cobbled court, the pediment on which their names were painted according to the custom of the Inns of Court, one ascended three flights of old, broad, low, sunken, Lordly-balustered stairs, until, under the roof, one faced a crazy dormer window surmounting two huge coal-lockers, either side of which was an ancient, heavy, carved oak door. Literal 'oaks' to be sported, for behind each was a second green-baize covered one, leading directly, without hall or lobby, into the long low-roofed main apartment with panelled walls and casement-windows extending the whole length of one side, and looking out upon the charming garden, now no more. The panelling, incidentally, was when they took over a bilious green, but they soon covered that with a more appropriate chocolate.

The rest of the 'suite' consisted of two inconsiderable bedrooms and a kitchenette so wee as barely to accommodate the unwieldy bulk of their charlady. There was no bathroom – a flat tin tub kept under one of the beds had to suffice, failing which the Holborn Public Baths – and no 'privy' save a communal six thrones across the cobbled courtyard.

Yet it was heaven.

Dürer was the god of Ken's idolatry at that stage, and, the whole place being so appropriate, they founded such schemes of decoration as their slender means allowed upon cheap German woodcuts of that master craftsman's work.

Lewis, who had been an engineer with the Positive Organ Co. before reaching theatres via school mastering, was every kind of a mechanic; luckily Ken had taken carpentry as an 'extra' at all his schools, and together they constructed, among other things, a panelled window seat, austere cushions atop, to run the whole length of their casements. Their electric lights, as soon as they got them, were encased in aged, Holy Family stable-lanterns from the

Caledonian Market, where they also managed to pick up a gate-leg table, wag-at-the-wall clock, a set of coffin stools, and (for thirty pieces of silver) the case of an elderly grand piano, to which Lewis miraculously applied innards. Stained boards, cheap rugs, very few pictures, stacks of books, and it was a home. A real home too. Ken was no doubt a callow youth with, maybe, possibilities. Lewis was more than ten years older, and the facts that he was so darn nice and that Ken was devoted to him made it a pretty good combination.

Lewis kept Ken in order, taught him to shave, lent him money, made him work at writing, saw to it that Ken had regular meals, ticked him off when needed, and generally brought him up in the way that he should go. They never had a wry word. They knew each other's people and each other's incomes; they couldn't have played each other's acting parts, and did not token to the same type of girl, so never criss-crossed those ways either.

Besides, if one wanted the flat for an afternoon, or the other did, the other one cleared off without demur, which was only seldom, for neither of the two was in love, and in those days sex, as such, irked neither of them too much.

It is true that at the Drury Lane Theatre there was one *fillette*, whose fascinating perky profile and adorable twinkling legs habitually dragged Ken to her entrance wing in Act 1, when he wasn't on stage, and made it rather a thrill to take her back to Clifford's Inn, to tea on matinee days now and then, but that wasn't a love affair or the other thing, so to speak. Just practice.

Childhood Memories of My Father

For the first ten years of my life, my father was 'Big Time'. He loved every minute of being in the limelight, and why not! But, as far as I can remember, we did not see a lot of him, what with filming abroad a lot and Sandy's to run! When he was home though, on odd weekends, special days or holidays, we had fun. He was a jolly person, always making jokes and always giving his whole attention to us children when we were together.

I can remember some Sundays – when we were living in the country, at Kings Langley, Hertfordshire – we would go to church on Sunday mornings. (Not Mum, who was left at home to cook the lunch!) We took Fossie (our dog at the time) with us and tied her up outside the church with a stern, 'Stay there, we won't be long.' Fossie was always good, and over the moon when we eventually came out. Then it was off to a pub for a well-earned drink! I remember this period quite vividly. I was sent to boarding School when I was five years old: Kings Langley Priory, later to become the first Rudolf Steiner school in England. It was OK. My brothers had been there some years before, as it was co-ed. It was a very unconventional place, where religion was taboo and everyone was vegetarian – most unusual for the time. In the huge grounds of the school were cows, ponies, donkeys, ducks and hens, all left to wander free. Only the goats were tethered, to stop them eating everything! We all had our own little gardens, where we could grow the flowers we liked – marigolds and asters amongst others – but the gardens had to be fenced off to keep the animals out. It was almost a home from home, and I have many happy memories of it.

I remember Dad coming to take me out one day. We spent the morning at Sandy's and later walked down Piccadilly, seeing Lord Beaverbrook, who had recently moved to London from his native Canada and had already bought and sold control of Rolls-Royce, quickly becoming a newspaper tycoon in the process by buying the *Evening Standard* and *Daily Express*, amongst others. Max Aitken was regarded as the first Baron of Fleet Street and one of the most powerful men in Britain, whose newspapers could make or break anyone!

We saw him across the road: 'Hello, Max', 'Hello, Ken.' Yes these were wonderfully happy days; Dad knew just about everyone. To a young girl of about eight, this really was something. Many people greeted him, so we never got very far quickly, but I didn't mind. 'And this is my daughter...' he would say. That was nice to hear and a big thrill.

We would sometimes go to the local shops, Dad meticulously jotting down each item needed on a pad and crossing them off before we left the shops. I can see him doing it now! List-making is something I also do and cannot do without! He always chatted to everyone, including dogs – 'Morning, dog' – and this is something I do to this day as well. Friendliness costs you nothing, and people seemed so pleased to see us, always stopping for a chat. There was no TV in those days, of course, but the radio kept everyone in touch with what was going on in the world, and the cinemas were always full. This was around 1928–30, by the way; everything was so different then.

Later, when I was about eleven, the marital problems between my parents seemed to pass over my head and I remember staying with Dad and Julie (his lady friend) on weekends at their charming little cottage in Waltham St Lawrence, Berkshire, no problem! I can also remember many summer holidays when Dad would rent a cottage for a whole month at numerous nice resorts that we all loved, such as St Margaret's Bay near Dover, Kent.

There were no holidays abroad in those days, although we did pop over to France when Dad was filming there. One of his films was called *Aristide Pujol*, which I was in! Fonder are the memories of Christmas time, when we played the usual games of the time including Rummy, Head, Body and Legs, and Consequences, amongst others. Yes, all these things made for a happy childhood; no regrets.

Stage, Screen and Sandwiches

The bar was filled to capacity and the air hummed with animated conversation and warm-hearted joviality. Did I say 'bar'? Yes, a sandwich bar: 25 Oxendon Street in London's West End, nestling behind the Prince of Wales Theatre, just off Piccadilly Circus – the first of its kind in England! The brainchild of actor, author and play producer Kenelm Foss, it was definitely the place to be seen in 1925. Kenelm Foss had just returned from New York, where he had produced and directed on Broadway a play starring John Barrymore (famous matinee idol of that era). Ken was already a household name in London, having acted in and produced numerous plays to much acclaim, including Chekhov's *The Cherry Orchard*, its first showing in Europe, and *Magic*, especially written for him by G K Chesterton. He had run the Glasgow Repertory Theatre for three years and been the mainstay of the burgeoning British film industry, acting and directing films, many of which he wrote himself. While in New York, he had seen 'eating joints' serving only sandwiches and coffee (probably due to prohibition) – easy places to pop into, without the formality of a sit-down meal. *London could do with such places*, he thought, and he certainly had the know-how! The First World War was over, people were rejoicing and wanting something new and exciting to happen, the theatres were full of light entertainment, revues and music halls were all the rage, and the public wanted to forget the past four years. Yes, this was the time! So, with a little help from all his many theatrical friends, plus technicians and out-of-work stage hands and scene builders he knew from his stage and screen work, it all started and 'Sandy's' was created. But wait, I'm jumping the gun. I think I should start at the beginning, when Ken (my father) started on the stage a few years before, back in 1904.

How It All Began: 1904–11

How it all began, as far as the theatre is concerned at any rate, was Ken being taken away from his public school at sixteen by his father as a punishment for having caricatured him and his fellow dignitaries of the Borough Council branch in the local paper. His father, of course, was the Mayor of Croydon and also a prominent lawyer. This may seem to have little to do with a stage career, but it actually plunged Ken prematurely into a profession in which he soon found he was quite unable to make a living – that of a black and white draughtsman.

To eke out the extremely slender allowance with which his father sent him to Coventry, he had to seek the help of his uncle, George R Foss, who was able by means of his stage connections to obtain for him a 'walk-on' part in a London theatre (The Court).

Do not imagine that he regretted or regarded as wasted that former time spent trying to earn a living by his pencil. It, and his failure at it, were like every other setback that had ever happened to him: invaluable in his training to become a competent producer of plays. From then on, he decided to invent and design his own scenes before the artist had ever heard of them, and the make-up for artists before they were engaged in their parts, to say nothing of such costumes as may have been required, before finally deciding which professional designer should receive the kudos on the programme. But if the 'walk-on' itself was a milestone, it was under the celebrated Vedrenne-Barker season at The Court theatre in London that he really began to excel.

That first production of Granville Barker's was a Greek play and the manner in which he managed to interest his producer is worth relating. The Greek warriors, or shepherds or whatever they were, were told to strip off all their clothes and to try to appear as natural as possible. His fellow 'supers' or 'walk-on' actors donned brownish tights and vests to represent sunburnt limbs. He, on the other hand, decided to paint his whole body all over with tea! For twenty minutes he had to stand in the centre of the stage while Granville Barker and Professor Gilbert Murray discussed whether they dare let him go on like that or not. Eventually they decided that he could! In so doing, he had forced himself upon the powers that be, with the consequence that his engagement was renewed, and there, under that historic regime, he remained until its premature demise.

He could not have had any better training, for in that period it was impressed indelibly on the mind of an enthusiastic and ambitious student of drama that one vital lesson of the theatre was to have courage and back one's own opinion. In those years he learned to loathe the obvious and distrust the normal, and incidentally, out of the great admiration he had for his employer and his work, he assimilated his technique as a play producer.

But do not let it be suggested, however, that he was a great success in those days. He was not, but he was learning and realising his ambition. He was a failure as a stage manager, and was the most unsatisfactory assistant any producer ever had, but he found what he was really good at in those early days and strenuous times: he had the knack of decorating and finishing a stage scene! Barker only had to say, 'And what I want is a characteristic suburban drawing room! 65/- a week rent.' And instead of him having to detail each piece of furniture or picture, he knew that Ken would know what he meant and was sufficiently insightful and imaginative to know what to do, and that he could rely on the complete room being there and right at the dress rehearsal!

He hardly ever altered anything Ken did in that particular line and used to swear that my father was quite invaluable. Certainly since he had been producing for himself he had never met with a stage manager to whom he could trust the selection of a single rug or curtain without a qualm.

But he had pulled himself out of a rut, so when Alfred Wareing, who had founded the Glasgow Repertory, came to Barker at his wit's end for a producer who *was* one and at the same time inexpensive, Barker thought that a flair for stage direction, coupled perhaps with some rudimentary intelligence he may have observed, were close enough akin to stage producing generally to enable him to risk recommending my father for the post.

So that was his first introduction to becoming a producer of plays! And during that time of scene-shifting and walk-on parts at 'His Majesty's', he noticed, admired and met 'E' (Elizabeth Gilson). She too was acting in small but significant parts to much acclaim in 1906. They married on 1 July, 1907, honeymooned at Lake Lucerne – a combined wedding gift from both families – and then came back to reality, living in sparsely-furnished rooms because they had so little income. Their first son, Felix, was born early in 1908, but sadly died six months later of gastroenteritis.

It was about this time that Granville Barker suggested that Ken should go to Glasgow to help run the Repertory Theatre, and although he was elated to receive such a wonderful opportunity he found it difficult to decide so soon after Felix's death. Elizabeth said he should go and she would follow directly, once he had found suitable accommodation. Meanwhile, she would go and stay with her mother and sisters for a while in Clapham. But, just before he went, while visiting friends in Hampstead, they noticed a tiny curio shop in Perrin's Court to let! Elizabeth fell in love with it straight away and thought she would like to run it, with the help of her sister Nell, while my father was in Glasgow. It would also serve to ease her sorrow by giving her something positive to do.

They became quite excited about the project and Dad promised to see the owner next morning, having wired Wareing that he would be a couple of days late arriving. They became excited about what they were going to sell; they had a few quite good pieces of cameos, ornaments and bits and pieces given to them on numerous occasions, and my father could think of lots of crockery and suchlike stored in a shed at his parents' home in Croydon, never used and just going to waste. He would also go to dealers to see what he could get and maybe collect some odd bits of small decorative furniture that was all the rage at that time.

They could not afford much – a crazy idea, really – but one never knew. They were complete amateurs with no commercial knowledge of running a business, and this they were to find out soon enough, after agreeing to lease the shop for a year – not a good move!

Things sold very slowly, or not at all, or they sold for less than they paid for them or were worth – all until my father had an urgent wire from Wareing, as things were desperate. So he took the first train to Glasgow to start an amazing new stage in his life (1909–11) and no one could deny that he received a thorough grounding in his newfound profession. During the three years he spent at the Repertory Theatre in Glasgow, they had a new play every Monday morning and nearly all the plays were masterpieces. Nor were they 'slung' on in the manner of the old stock companies, for the only means of success was to compete with the musical comedies and popular successes that the other two theatres in the town were showing.

Meanwhile, back at the shop! Although things were difficult, Elizabeth and her sister enjoyed their time there and found that the people liked their decorative furniture and wished they had more to sell. After a while, Elizabeth found that she was expecting again – not a good time, but a blessing in some ways, for she would have another child to care for soon after losing Felix such a short time before. Also, the lease on the shop was about to expire, so to close it then was probably the best option.

Glasgow

Meanwhile, Dad was over the moon in his new life in Scotland, enjoying every minute in the whole wonderful environment of the theatre. There were, naturally, some problems with being only a repertory theatre: they had very little stock of scenery and, with a necessarily inexpensive cast, they had to borrow and beg every piece of furniture and ornament from local tradespeople, who were as enthusiastic about the Repertory Theatre as those involved in it were.

Even though everyone enjoyed being part of the company, work was, unfortunately, spasmodic due to the different seasons. So Dad turned to writing to eke out money to live on, which he would send to Elizabeth. In that time he wrote a novel, *Till Our Ship Comes In* – a very apt title! (This was, incidentally, made into a very popular film at a later stage.) He also wrote a book of poems called *The Dead Pierrot*. Both of these became a vital part of his next assignment in life, when he was to return to London for another exciting step in his theatrical career.

At that time, my father had begun one of the busiest times in the theatre, but still managed to scrounge a couple of days to come down to Hampstead to settle things up at the shop, with a promise to return to Glasgow as quickly as possible. At Hampstead he had to contact an auctioneer with hopes of making a small profit on the remaining items they had left, and to settle up with the shop owner. The auction was a farce; they lost practically everything, not having any previous knowledge of running a shop or a business and especially because of his inability to supervise the arrangements of the auction catalogue.

His inexperience of commercial dealings was also partly responsible for the fact that their poor little bits and pieces were almost ignored, as these were the first on the list in the catalogue and were put up for auction before many of the bidders had arrived. Most of their things, for which they hoped so much, went at scandalously low prices, much less than they had paid for them or knew that they were worth. Ironically, the only thing they made a profit on was a hideous pseudo-antique chair that my father had always detested. They also had to pay the auctioneer and helpers for their so-called dues; after all had been paid they were left with nothing and in debt! The whole thing had been an absolute disaster.

But Dad regretted that the whole irony and pathos did not at that time come home to him, for his mind was back in Glasgow and on his mild 'affairs' with Pippa, Irene Rooke, and his flirtations with numerous members of the fairer sex in the theatre, which afterwards added to his guilty feelings for the lack of communication over long periods of time with his family.

He had to return to Glasgow and Elizabeth returned to Clapham with her sister. But it was so busy at the Royalty, what with rehearsals and running the theatre almost single-handed (as Wareing wasn't well), that he was hardly ever home in his digs in the evenings, so not much harm was done. Irene Rooke was due to return to Manchester (having been loaned to Glasgow, as they were short of female actresses at the Royalty), so things soon settled down somewhat.

But my father wasn't actually very well; he was depressed and had eczema on his face – a nervous complaint, according to the doctor whom he visited when worried. The doctor, a kindly Scot who refused to take a fee (realising Dad's lack of money), put him back on his feet again by suggesting a lotion for his face and a 'soother' for his depression. Lucky for him, as he had nearly been turned out of his lodgings by his landlady for having an obnoxious disease!

Meanwhile, things were still busy at the theatre, although, when there was a lull, his kind management more than once gave him permission to accept offers of productions in London. It was only when two of these productions had been stolen from him – that is to say, while every particular of the production remained the same as he intended, his name on the posters as producer was subtitled by that of other interested parties as soon as he was safely back in Glasgow – he resolved to avoid such barefaced fraud (for which there was no possible redress) in the future by putting himself in a position where the policy of the theatre was controlled, and the billings checked by himself.

All these beginnings of his might sound facile, or easy perhaps, but they were not. In the early stages, he was always quite shamefully underpaid for the work he did and the enthusiasm he brought to it. In the long periods between engagements, he more than once quite literally starved! He was constantly laughed at as a lunatic, and his unwavering belief in his own ability to make good eventually was 'pooh-poohed'. Later, they smilingly assured him that they always knew he had it in him, and he smiled too. For that is the fate of the individual artist – more, it is his triumph!

During all this time, normality ruled in the theatre until Elizabeth wired him to say that the babies (twins this time) were due to arrive shortly. So, he had to ask for more days off again to dash home for the birth (9 September, 1910) of two more sons, Jonathan and David. He soon had to return as promised to start rehearsals for the Christmas shows and present a triple bill of one-act plays in the meantime. It was as simple as that: either stay with Elizabeth, or work in Glasgow for money for all four of them to live on.

My father was still, by the way, only twenty-five years old. Elizabeth was to follow with the boys as soon as he could find suitable rooms for them. Meanwhile, she would stay with her mother and sisters (again) – under the circumstances a much better place to be.

Before Miss Rooke left for her Christmas break, Dad invited her to watch the triple-bill rehearsals, and this, for what it is worth, was her opinion of them: 'All the plays exceptional, well-produced and especially the interiors and scenery (Ken's speciality).' She knew none who could have done it better. The acting, too, she likewise approved of, Henry Ainley being 'exceptionally good' in one of the leads. In one of the plays, *Columbine*, Dad played a small part, as there was no other actor available or suitable. He played the character with a lurch and a stutter. He had intended it to be funny and pathetic at the same time, and to his credit he got it right. On the first night, he had a teeny triumph when his first appearance got a round of applause.

He would have liked Elizabeth to see the triple bill, but it was just not possible. She wired him soon after to tell him about the article called 'What is a producer?' He had written it hastily six months previously and dispatched it to the *New Age* newspaper proprietor before he was really satisfied with it, because they declared they wanted to print it immediately.

Now, after this long interval, and when he had almost forgotten its very existence, it had at last appeared. He rushed out to buy a copy, filled, he could not deny, with considerable elation! Although he was not paid for it – although his name did not appear – it was an article by *him*, in a paper of some distinction! The first fruit of his aspirations! And it was not such bad stuff either. He knew that as he read it in the street on his way back to the house, and looking at it now his opinion was still the same. It was clear, concise sense and very readable! All his colleagues participated in his enthusiasm and bought copies at the earliest opportunity.

Later, my father was able to nip back to London for a few days to see Elizabeth and the boys before the Christmas play got under way. The babies were so different after just a few weeks. David was a big chubby chap with red cheeks and a big smile, Jon-Jon rather puny beside him, pale and thin. But they were both doing well, much to Elizabeth's credit. Poor, patient, faithful dear, how strong she was in their fraught, unsettled lives! Dad had another quick couple of days for Christmas with the family and then had to return to spend New Year's Eve and Day on his own – or so he thought.

New Year's Day, 1911, my father woke early, got in touch with the Wareings, wishing them Happy New Year, then walked all around Glasgow in glorious sunshine. He felt better for it as he had spent New Year's Eve on his own, feeling sorry for himself and wanting company. Suddenly he saw Irene Rooke, who lodged just a few doors away, coming out of her gate.

Dad hadn't seen her for some time, as she had been home for her Christmas break and had just returned to Glasgow that morning. They were pleased to see each other. They supped together that evening and also on numerous other occasions. They found they had so many subjects and tastes in common and became quite intimate again in a free and easy, boyish sort of comradeship. They so much enjoyed being together whenever they had the opportunity, but of course Ken felt guilty – he always did!

Later, Dad decided that, things being as they were – the theatre being busy at that time of year, and what with having to traipse backwards and forwards to London so often – there was nothing to prevent his whole ménage joining him at the earliest opportunity. There was just the small problem of finding suitable lodgings. This proved easier said than done, as landladies were not all that amenable to accommodating two small babies as well as their parents! Eventually, he managed to find a kindly person who took pity on him.

The place was not ideal – stuffy and over-furnished with very unsuitable furniture – but the landlady was a motherly soul and took to the babies straight away. As soon as they arrived, and of her own accord, she borrowed a cradle from her sister for one of the boys. The other would sleep in the pram.

Elizabeth arrived on Friday 10 March, 1911. After some doubt and correspondence, they had decided that they sadly could not afford their own special little nursemaid's (Ethel) return fare. So, although she was an excellent worker and would be heartbroken at not coming with them as she was so fond of the boys, they had instead to engage a similar girl by the week in Glasgow, but with the promise that they would re-engage Ethel upon returning to London. The consequence was that poor Elizabeth had somehow to manage the twins on that awful journey alone. It was a matter of amazement to my father that she managed it!

But there they were, the three of them, as the train steamed into the Central: in a fuzzy carriage, the two little chaps sitting each end of a corner seat, dressed in purple coats and woolly leggings, both as good as gold; the prettiest, most touching sight one could ever conceive. Fortunately, they had found a good guard (though my father fancied that most guards were good); he had thoroughly earned his five bob. He had locked them in, looking in from time to time to see that all was well, brought Elizabeth tea in the morning and even warmed the boys' bottles! They taxied to the rooms in Stanley Street while the new maid wheeled the pram along the pavement. And as they did so, in spite of the strangeness that they had begun to look for between them after partings – however short – Ken found that out of the chaos of his unsettled, unhealthy life, their coming shed a sort of hope of better, happier times.

After settling in, the next morning they went out shopping for a few essential things: a tin bath for bathing the boys and numerous bits and pieces not provided at the lodgings – although the landlady did lend them a low chair. There was a lull in rehearsals at the Royalty, so my father was eager to do something to earn a little more money. He started to write his first play, *The Average Man*; he prepared and cast *Romeo and Juliet* for immediate production at Wareing's request; he bought copies of his 'Producer' article and dispatched them to numerous patrons whom he thought might be interested.

In an idle moment he wrote to an agent, Eden Payne of Manchester, and to the Stage Society about future work. On some evenings, Dad and Elizabeth went to the local music hall, the Alhambra. Once they saw Pavlova dancing her pièce de resistance, *The Dying Swan*. She had recently defected from Russia and was now doing a one-woman show round the main cities of Britain; later she was to settle in Hampstead.

My father continued to rehearse *Romeo and Juliet*, when all of a sudden, without any warning, the theatre 'burst', meaning things came to a sudden and complete halt until further notice for lack of funds. So, since this would deprive them of eight weeks' salary, it came as a dreadful shock. Could they by any possibility have known then, Elizabeth and the twins would never have spent all that money coming to Glasgow!

The only thing to do now was to leave Glasgow yet again. Perhaps stay with Elizabeth's mother – again! They decided to look for somewhere in the country for a couple of months as a sort of holiday, where Dad could maybe write to try and earn a few pence to keep things going. He had always yearned to live in Elstree, having visited it some years before and found it rather charming. So Elstree it was to be, as long as they could find somewhere suitable and cheap.

Leaving Glasgow, they stopped at Elizabeth's mother's for a while, but it was too cramped with all their ménage there.

Luckily, a friend of Dad's lent him his flat in Hampstead for a few weeks while my father and Elizabeth's sister, Nell, looked for somewhere suitable in Elstree. Hopefully Dad would find some freelance work to tide them over.

Suddenly, after nearly a month (2 May), my father was summoned to an interview with Frederick Whelan of the Stage Society, with whom he was now quite 'hail fellow well met', and informed him that the play, *The Married Woman*, was postponed and that the next production was to be Chekhov's *The Cherry Orchard*. Dad was asked if he would undertake that for them, or whether he would prefer to retain his call upon *The Married Woman* in such time as it should be done. Thus, with the recollection of the last three weeks' salary, and although he had already done all the spadework of the Frenalds' play by preparing it elaborately on paper for rehearsal, my father accepted the Chekhov play with thanks, though he knew no more of the author than that his friend Calderman had once translated one of his plays, *The Seagull*, which had well nigh wrecked the theatre!

Calderman had also, Dad learnt, prepared a version of *The Cherry Orchard* and had indeed submitted it to the Stage Society. Nevertheless, it was not his version of the play that was to be performed, but one by a Mrs Garrett, a Russian translator of Tolstoy. Her work had been selected instead of Calderman's not because of her notability as a translator from Russian, but because her copy had been submitted to the society seven years before, while Calderman's had grown dusty in the office for a mere matter of a year! Calderman's copy was far superior according to my father, when he eventually read it.

Dad read the script, or rather, two acts of it, in bed that night – and reread them to be sure that he had not misunderstood. The other two he saved for the next day and he came down to breakfast with an all-too-seldom-experienced sensation: that he had unwittingly stumbled on a masterpiece! It was the play of his lifetime! There could be no manner of doubt as he reread it again and was more enthusiastic than ever! He gave it to Elizabeth to read, who declared it was nonsense, but he was so sure about it that her opinion didn't matter to him!

There had always been such controversy regarding the play; so many differences of opinion. A typical Russian story sometimes not fully understood by different nationalities. A typical objection launched against the play was as thus: in the ensemble scene, 'So unlikely,' they said, 'that any collection of sane people should sit down and talk at three o'clock in the morning!' My father, for his part, had not found it at all improbable at the time he read it, but, if he had, Mrs. Garrett had an answer that would dispose firmly of that objection: probable or not, Russians do! At a time of unusual excitement, as that was, they would not go to bed at all, as likely as not. The more my father was involved with this play, the more it was, in his view, a play on the same level of excellence as Ibsen's *Wild Duck*.

More controversy! Ken felt he had to state his view to Hertz and Whelan, the presenters, and to declare that if his production did not suit the Society, then the Society had better get someone else to do it! But the Society agreed with him, and so that was the way it was produced.

Unquestionably, the most awkward task for Dad was his attitude towards Calderman who, he felt strongly, had a distinct grievance. He had read his version, and there was no question at all that it was the better of the two. The actors' aspect towards the play was most interesting. Some of them had not understood it when it was produced. Franklyn Dyall, Nigel Playfair and Mary Jerald all thought it was drivel for six rehearsals and then saw what a masterpiece it was. The only fly in the ointment was the leading lady, Katherine Pole. She was the damning of his labours. She did not understand her place in the play in the least. She was a schoolmarm and bored them all to tears. 'Oh, to have had Ellen Terry!'

George Bernard Shaw, on my father's first meeting with him, sat beside him all through the dreadful dress rehearsal, writing voluminously when the curtain was down or nothing was happening. His opinion was that Sunday would be the most historic first night in England since the production of *The Doll's House*. On the first night, the audience sat stupefied during the first act, grew restless during the second, and began to leave during the third. Bunston forgot his words at the opening of the fourth scene and, while endeavouring to remember them, drunkenly staggered about. Calderman, taking this for my father's business, flew into a white heat, insulted Whelan (poor little innocent Whelan) volubly, and left the building.

All through the last act, the rest of the audience followed his example as far as the departure was concerned, and some of them regarded it as the abuse of Whelan! 'Biggest rot I ever listened to!' my father heard a genial military gentleman remark. Those who stayed hooted and hissed loudly. The last scene, Madame Raneky's final one, was inaudible. There was silence for the first death scene, but some applause for the actor who played it, and after that a volley of hisses for the piece.

My father had supper with Whelan afterwards, who told him, 'No one seemed to like it.' Fortunately, he too saw how little that mattered! There was splendid work from the players and even Miss Pole rose to the occasion at the end. Dad had got good furniture and the nursery scene was fine. The band, as if by a miracle, was exactly right, the crowd better than he had hoped for, and he was quite contented with his part and was glad to report that he convinced the powers that be of his point of view.

Mrs Garrett was delighted; Eden Payne was in her box and he too was enthusiastic and held out more tangible hopes of Dad joining them in the autumn. He received congratulations also from Whelan and Hertz, and formally from the council of the Society. The newspapers – the few of them that understood it – were enthusiastic. The *Westminster*, the *Star* and the *New Age* were papers he saw, all of which were very polite to him personally.

After the entire *Cherry Orchard* charade, my father was very tired and needed a restful time. Hopefully Elstree would do the trick; he and Nell went to have a look around (while Elizabeth looked after the boys) and just by chance found the ideal place. It was the end of a row of cottages, so had only one lot of neighbours, the other side being just a hedge separating them from the beautiful gardens of Elstree School. And it was quite cheap too, only 8/6d a week rent! They moved in on 11 July, 1911.

The van was late in coming with their bits of furniture (that had been stored at Ken's parent's house in Croydon for some time), which meant they were all at their wit's end – and he should have been at the matinee of *The Married Woman*! The house was unfurnished, by the way, and rather big, so their pathetic excuse for furniture looked rather out of place in the largish rooms. Some kind neighbour lent them two large cushions for the boys to sleep on (so good of them); Elizabeth's mother and sister came more or less every weekend to stay with them and were obviously a great help with the boys. They also brought the family dog, Lazzy, with them, having looked after it whenever they were in Glasgow or other unsuitable places for dogs. He was a very amenable animal, but loved the boys, and they him. My father was still hoping to get an assignment in Manchester, promised to him some time before. He heard the next morning that they would let him know within a few days! It was certainly nice, so to speak, to be in the open air for a while!

Soon after they arrived, they noticed a flower show in the grounds of the magnificent house of Lord Alderham, which they all went to. It was an exceedingly hot summer, almost stifling in the middle of the day. By this time the twins were nearly nine months old, crawling everywhere and into everything. They put the boys into a baby show, but sadly did not get a mention. The local doctor, who was judging the show, had been very rude to Elizabeth as soon as they got there, and nothing, said she, would ever induce her to have him in her house. Everyone agreed he was an overbearing brute of a man, and Ken agreed also. He had disliked the look of the doctor – disliked and distrusted him right from the start – but they enjoyed the show otherwise and the glorious grounds. They had re-engaged their original little nursemaid, Ethel. She was so pleased to see the twins again, and they her! Time rolled along quite happily, with my father doing the odd bits of writing and endless enquiries for work, money, as usual, being almost non-existent. Elizabeth and her mother popped back to London for a couple of days, but were returning on 18 August with Nell.

The Picnic: 20 August, 1911

That fateful morning, my father had received by post a letter informing him that he had not got the Manchester theatrical engagement that he had so set his heart on and really thought he would get.

Lewis Casson had definitely accepted the offer, leaving Dad to realise the palpable truth that Elizabeth had been right about Payne (his agent). She had never liked him nor trusted him. Payne had practically promised the job and, for all his friendliness, had not had the decency to drop Dad a postcard to say he was not wanted after all; and all this although three months had elapsed, instead of the fortnight he had mentioned in the first place!

This, of course, was not the first time such a thing had happened to him, but somehow he was not yet inured to being treated like dirt. It would come no doubt, but where in all life, in the name of God, was there a place for him?

My father was utterly sick at heart – he was, by his own admission, interminably slow at writing, and could not see how he could ever have six months to write a book himself without money troubles. So, for one more pitiful time, he started to look for theatrical work again. The Stage Society had given him hope of joining their ranks in the autumn, but in the meantime he needed money, and fast! Barker and Wareing were the only people to get him work, so he sat down to write to them – letters that took the writer all morning to compose. He supposed he had counted so much on the Manchester job because it meant so much to them (Elizabeth and he) – £6 a week (he had hoped for £8), and a year's contract, which meant £150 put by in a year and a half.

Elizabeth arrived back at the cottage on the morning of 20 August, 1911. It was a lovely day, so they decided to have a picnic on Stanmore Common where they had been numerous times before. They found a clearing under some pine trees where they usually sat. Coming, they joked about always bringing books and never reading them, but today they were determined to read. Ethel had been warned that she might have to look after the boys more than usual. My father brought some magazines too, hoping to find some that might be interested in his articles.

The boys were with them at lunch, or at least at the beginning of lunch, for David behaved so badly, crawling all over the tablecloth and insisting on picking at everyone's food, that he had to be removed, howling. He was as healthy that day as anyone had seen him. They saw very little of the children for the next couple of hours; Jon was asleep and David was with Ethel. After tea, as was their usual custom, they dressed the boys in their nightclothes and placed them down on the ferns beside them. David always looked the fat, chubby baby; Jon, of another world, almost like an elf, he was so fragile. David was a Reuben's cupid.

As they walked home, someone remarked that David was rather pale. It didn't excite much comment, as it had been a hot day and it was near his bedtime. That evening at supper they heard him crying – quite usual; most babies wake in the night and are frightened. Nell went up to him and found he had been sick. They transferred him to sleep with Elizabeth, while Jon was put in David's crib. Once or twice in the night he woke up crying, but, unlike the sickness, it did not seem unusual. At 5 a.m. on Monday 21 August, Elizabeth asked my father to come and see him, as she thought he'd better go for a doctor.

In her bed he found a child he could not have recognised: he had black sunken eyes, thin cheeks and a generally unearthly look. He was extremely worried and rode to Bushey instantly to telephone a doctor he had been given the name of. He explained the symptoms, but the doctor 'pooh-poohed' their fears. This sudden change of a child's appearance was the commonest sign of diarrhoea, a most common complaint in hot weather! (Sunstroke was suspected but never proved.) Should he come to see the child? For Elizabeth's sake, Dad said, 'Yes!' The doctor came and prescribed castor oil; Dad rode to Stanmore to get some.

The next morning, he looked after Jon while Elizabeth saw to David. Ethel was due to depart for her holiday that evening, so there was much to be done. They did all they could to help with David and were concerned with the little chap's discomfort. My father thought Elizabeth was worrying unnecessarily, though he thought it natural after little Felix.

Early the next morning, David was still no better, troubled either with sickness or diarrhoea, but clearly in pain and with an incessant thirst. He yawned and clearly wanted to go to sleep but seemed unable to do so.

My father telephoned the doctor again; he was most irritable with Dad for disturbing him. Babies, he declared, could go without sleep for very long periods. He would struggle to sit up, but couldn't on his own, so they lay him back again. He would be there for a few moments, sucking on his comforter.

The top of his head was hot and wet and he was so altered that, in sober truth, one could not recognise him. Elizabeth came up to make him comfortable, change his clothes, change his position in bed and see if he could sleep. Today his ribs showed far too clearly – he was wasting away, a sight to make them shudder. Elizabeth said that when he was away she had had to watch little Felix looking five times as terrible as that.

Ethel was to go on holiday that evening and stated categorically that it was her right to do so! One couldn't understand why anyone would want to leave a child in that much pain (and one who she was supposed to care for), but she did! David continued to deteriorate and it was pitiful to see and hear his dreadful discomfort. My father called the doctor once again; he was out, but would be told to come as soon as he returned.

Two hours went by, and in desperation my father went out to see if there was anyone else who could help. By now it was after nine o'clock at night and everyone in Elstree was in bed, or so it seemed. He knocked up a neighbour who said the nearest garage was in Radlett, a few miles away. He was just about to cycle there when he saw the lights of the doctor's car in the road. They took him upstairs, the doctor murmuring the whole time about the unusual symptoms of the case.

After looking at David he said, 'What this child needs is a nice dose of castor oil!' Elizabeth gave him a look that was almost a laugh of derision. Whether this spurred the doctor to sound him, one couldn't say, but at any rate he did so and knew instantly that David was dying... That he was, in fact, dead.

Elizabeth sent my father out of the room. He stood there where Jon was sleeping till she came and told him. The poor, stupid little doctor passed the time telling anecdotes of similar cases. Neither of them listened. He had no understanding whatsoever of the case, and he *knew* he had known nothing whatsoever about it! Talking it over afterwards, both of them found they felt quite sorry for him, and for the second time they both had to pay by sacrificing a child to the ignorance and incompetence of the medical profession.

Did my father believe in God? Although God took away nothing of him personally, my father could see, in a combination of circumstances that ended in the death of his son David, a plot to destroy a beautiful thing that was a source of pure joy to several poor, hard lives. The incident could have happened nowhere else but in an isolated village like Elstree! Your logical Christian would say that, for the first time in their married life, they had decided to spend the summer in a remote district. God sent them to Elstree so that David might die for lack of a competent doctor near at hand.

The colonial doctor, whom they had taken a dislike to at the Flower Show, was an excellent children's doctor, they were informed. It is clear, therefore, from the Christian point of view, that God made him rude to Elizabeth at the sports day so that David should die for the lack of his services.

Again, a Mrs Sanderson at School House knew much more about babies and could have helped them, and they would have been in touch with her if the school had not happened to have chicken pox – sent by God to put a barrier between them and the only person who could have saved their little son! God it was, perhaps, who sent them; put it into their minds to go to a place where they had no friends. God who sent them the hottest summer for twenty or thirty years at David's most susceptible age! God who put it into the hearts of Nell and her mother to leave that Sunday night instead of stopping until the next day, as they had thought of doing, which might have saved him. God who made Ethel's holiday happen on that day and God who left them both in intolerable, unbelievable bleeding misery. No one cares; we just drift on and there is no purpose in it. The finest, purest, best thing in his life, the one brightness in poor old Nell's miserable, hopeless existence, was just snapped off carelessly, like a nettle by a passing stick. Elizabeth – that wonderful Elizabeth – who was just a nurse, not a mother on that nightmare of a day, and did not become a mother again until they lay on the floor in the bedroom for what rest they could get on that horrible night.

A nurse had come the night before to lay David out. He was not allowed to remain in his bed where he had died, poor little chap, but was laid on the chest of drawers in Ethel's room. He still wore the woolly clothes that Elizabeth had put on him for his ride to the hospital. Jon Jon slept the night with Fanny, the next-door neighbour's niece. The next morning found them dull and broken, glad for the things that had to be done, that their minds might be occupied. They had thought of cremation, as neither of them cared for the thought of the little body lying in a dark coffin, but they had heard that it was most expensive, and my father found this to be true on enquiring at Golder's Green. He rode back to Elstree and arranged with the vicar and the undertaker that the funeral should take place there. He rode back to Elizabeth and Jon Jon sweet and charming, as if he realised their sorrow.

What a change comes over the human creature when it is dead! My father saw David for the first time since that awful morning, and there was, in the sight of him, no cause for weeping. He was beautiful, and David had never been beautiful! He was still, cold and clean – none of which was David. His hair lay smooth, as David's had never lain, and his features were refined and delicate, bearing no relation to the dear ones of my father's son.

He was not smiling as that little boy always was. Only by recollecting what had gone, by looking out of the window into the garden and remembering that dumpling who crawled there so happily – the little grub whose clothes and face and hands were never clean for long – made one close to tears and impotent cries against the cruelty and injustice of it all. But even then they did not entirely realise that he had gone. My father had to wire everyone to tell them of the death and the funeral.

Elstree had become loathsome to them all, so they decided to go straight to Croydon after the funeral and return only for their furniture. They left Nell, who had returned to look after Lazzy and their things, and headed for Croydon for the night. My father's mother opened the door and her inability to rise to the emotional crisis was so marked that they could not fail to notice it. The expression on her face as she opened the door led them to believe that she could not have heard the news. Even so, it was good to have some sort of family home still in existence. The only other people there were Dolly, who was matter-of-fact, which was good for them, and dear old 'Nurse' Harvey, on whose breast my father cried his stupid broken heart out, just as he had done – he remembered – a hundred times before when he was a young boy.

They left early the next morning, so as not to leave Nell in the cottage for too long, although she had Lazzy for company. Harvey looked on her as Jon Jon's protector; he was being bathed as they left. Harvey, Dolly and Aunt Moll all insisted on giving Dad money, which he would rather not have taken, but which, for all that, was particularly useful just then. Indeed, without it, they did not know how all the expenses could have been paid.

Back at the cottage they found a letter from Wareing. It asked my father to return to Glasgow if possible, naming a salary of £6, which was an advance of £1 on his previous one, and wanting him to produce Arnold Bennett's new play, *The Great Adventure*, on 18 September. They were glad to accept. Glasgow and the theatre were no longer unattractive to them. So much worse had happened to them since they were last there – and they had dreaded having to continue living at the house in Elstree, bound up with such recollections of David. This gave them the excuse to be rid of it, and it would be the first time my father had earned a salary without having to pay two rents!

Next day came flowers from everyone at Croydon, and from unknown neighbours two doors down. Later Ted (Ken's brother) came over – invaluable help to them in many ways – then Mrs Gilson, laden with flowers from herself, her son and daughter-in-law, and daughter.

The funeral was detestable! My father saw his dear little boy in a ridiculous and pretentious French white and silver box. Dad and Elizabeth carried him between them, from the chest of drawers in Ethel's room to the gate-legged table downstairs on which Felix had lain only a year before. Dad had stopped the tolling of the bell and the undertaker was himself to carry the little box on his shoulders. They had hoped they would reach the churchyard via the path that led from their cottage to the church, but the undertaker assured them that they would not be allowed to do so.

So through the village street they were made to go, first the undertaker with the little box on his shoulder, then both of them with flowers, hating the whole public business and feeling most uncomfortable. Then followed Ted, who was invaluable to them as the officiator, followed by Nell and her mother, also with flowers. Children ran quickly past them, obviously so that they might get ahead and have a good look backwards. Tradespeople peered inquisitively out of their windows and from their stalls. At the lynch gate they were met by the rector, and the service proceeded, a service so totally unsuited to the child for whom it was held. They found it an irksome, tedious, unreal affair and were heartily glad when it was over.

They went back to Ted's from Borehamwood – the news that the Mona Lisa had been stolen had come through that morning – and to soothe their minds, after a light meal, they went to the Queen's Hall to listen to Sir Henry Wood and his orchestra. The next morning they went back to Croydon to fetch Jon Jon and then back to Elstree to settle everything up, with the hope that they would never set foot in that part of the country again.

By then, my father was not feeling at all well and Elizabeth, although stronger than him in every situation, was not feeling in the best of health herself. The dreadful previous few days had obviously been the cause. Even Jon Jon seemed a little out of sorts. They went back to Elizabeth's mother's house this time, where Nell and Lazzy were waiting for them, as before. Within a few days they would be returning to Glasgow again. Depressed and despondent, my father could only think of Mr. McCawber's words: 'Something will turn up!' Something would turn up, but when?

Glasgow Again

Not having to return to Glasgow until 18 September (it was now the 8th), Dad and Elizabeth went back to Croydon for a few days before travelling to celebrate Jon Jon's birthday on the 9th. Celebrating was hardly on their minds, but he wouldn't understand as he was too young. They bought him a contraption for walking round the room in. He also had a small cake that he merely crumbled in his fingers.

After the birthday, lying in bed the next day, my father's mind turned to David again. It was useless blaming oneself for not having made enough of him on that last day. He had only occasionally paid him attention while he lay there and was ignored while Dad wrote and read. It was a useless business, but he could not stop himself and he asked nothing better than to die there and then – no melodramatics, no sentiment. He had not the spirit to live. But after three days lying there resting and supping on soup and Bovril, Dad regained his senses.

Elizabeth had not realised Dad had felt so bad, and Jon Jon being a little seedy had distracted her attention. Uncle George came to visit and gave him £10. Harvey nursed him for a day and a half until he recovered enough to think about getting back to Glasgow. Before that they would stay with some friends in Golder's Green, leaving Jon Jon at Croydon under Harvey's care. She would love that!

Next morning a letter came from Wareing saying that Arnold Bennett, the author of *The Great Adventure*, had insisted on Frank Vernon producing his play instead of my father, leaving it unclear whether they proposed to pay him for the two weeks money he would lose! However, he was to play a small part in the play. A most unsatisfactory affair altogether, and much worried was he with all the rent, bills and the fares to Glasgow. His money, including the £10 Uncle George had given him, was all accounted for and he had not enough to support them during the two weeks idleness!

Fortunately Wareing was coming down to London the next

day. Dad went to the station, impatiently waiting as the train was half an hour late (as usual). Wareing and his wife, when the train eventually arrived, were amicability itself. Dad had breakfast with them and, getting Wareing alone for a few minutes, he got him in a corner, where after wavering he agreed to meet my father halfway and pay him half salary for those first two weeks. Unsatisfactory – but better than nothing! The next day Dad met Wareing again and travelled on the city line for an inspection of probable players at the Little Theatre for work at the Royalty.

On 18 September, having collected Jon Jon from Croydon (Harvey was sad to see him go), and packed up their belongings, they were once again on their way to Glasgow. London, eighty-seven degrees in the shade; Glasgow, midwinter! That was the first impression they got on alighting from the train. This was a city (according to Dad), so utterly depressing that life seemed useless. Black gloom lay on them for the next few days. Jon Jon was the most cheerful of the party.

My father had written for the pleasant rooms they had once occupied before, but unfortunately these had already been booked by another of the theatre company (Breen), so they found themselves in rooms that, in the absence of anything remotely suggesting home, incensed the melancholy of the atmosphere.

There were many thoughts of David in the first few days. Actually, on reflection much of the Elstree stay had been happy and all of it a 'sunny' time. One could not help think of how he, the merry one of their party, would have made even these bare rooms seem bright, but Jon Jon, though no sort of a substitute, did his best.

Where to write? That was the question. Glasgow didn't seem to possess a public library. Their good landlady happened to have a small room in the attic that Dad could have for an extra 5/- a week, which he did. You bet! Their landlady, by the way, was Belgian and actually an exceedingly nice woman, but with no money, her husband dead and three children that were a handful. She had no help, so was cooking meals for all the lodgers, lunch and supper, as well as shopping, etc. She had no time for cleaning the house, so it was no wonder that Jon Jon got exceedingly grubby crawling around on the floor.

During the first week, Dad had time to make up his journal

and get straight for the literary work, when the weeks to spare came along. He had been told what part he had to play in *The Great Adventure of the Dying Valet*, and in Act 1, in which he impersonated the leading part, he would be on at the rise of the curtain and finished within ten minutes. Vernon, who was producing instead of my father, was, as he saw, a self-opinionated, posturing ignoramus, but, even so, most considerate to him, and never kept him hanging about.

The play, Dad thought, was rather boring and vulgar. Lloyd, who played the leading part, was totally unsuited for the role and Helen Haynes, who played the female lead, was only just capable (she actually went on to become a very well-known West End actress). His old friend, Percy Marment, was in the cast too, and incidentally acted for him in later years in London. Many actors started at the Royalty and were proud of it.

The next play to go on was now to be thought of and *The Return of the Prodigal* was decided upon. Breen would play the prodigal with Lloyd as Hern. My father suggested Miss Norman as Lady Farringford, the ill-bred aristocrat. But oh, what a deuce of a to-do! Miss Norman had never been so insulted in her life. She was appalled and would not play such a part, eventually producing a letter from Wareing that enabled her to evade my father's casting and, to her inconsiderable penalty, draw no salary till her next appearance should take place.

So Mrs Marment, who was cast as Mrs Pratt, was transferred to Lady Farringford and, after much consultation, Elizabeth was cast as Mrs Pratt! She was instantly ever-so-much concerned about clothes for the part (eventually provided out of Mrs Wareing's wardrobe) and especially an overcoat to replace her extremely shabby one, so they spent every free moment looking for a coat: it had to be grey – but not tweed – and it must fit her exactly; she could not wait to have one made. There were some obstacles in our race, apart from the leading one – Dad's views on what it cost! They searched every shop in Sauchiehall Street, but to no avail. Eventually she decided on having one made. It seemed a flimsy thing to my father, without warmth or anything else to recommend it, save a pink lining. When it was ready, she proceeded to swank around in it, before the company and before the rehearsals.

20–21 October, 1911

The week of the rehearsals went well, with Elizabeth enjoying her acting part and showing off her new clothes. They supped on the last night with a friend named Thompson, a well-to-do amateur photographer who took several photographs of them: my father lighting a cigar and Elizabeth standing and sitting against a white wall. The photos turned out to be nothing particular, they were disappointed to find, for Thompson had turned out wonderful things in that way in the past.

Thompson did actually lend my father *The Honeymoon*, Arnold Bennett's new play, which Dad liked but did not think a winner commercially. He also lent *The Wheel of Chance*; Dad was very interested as it was the only H G Wells book he had not read.

The next day, Dad went to Perth for a couple of days with an old friend, Harker, after all the stress of rehearsals of *The Return of the Prodigal*. Elizabeth would not come as she was acting in 'that play at the Royalty'. In his rooms, they had a pleasant lunch of eggs, bacon and home-made rolls. They got back on their old footing. Ken had forgotten that Harker was such a fine fellow and an extremely loveable one.

Another amazing thing happened that week. A large parcel arrived out of the blue, containing numerous books my father had sold years ago and, lo and behold, his Malvern drawing prize, received before he went to the Slade.

A bundle of Elizabeth's letters and numerous other items that he thought he would never have seen again, all from someone in the past who had shared digs with them years ago; someone who neither of them cared about! There was a note with the parcel saying he had found them on a bookstall in Chancery Lane! They could only suppose they had got mislaid or lost in one of their numerous moves. My father never thought he would have to be grateful to that man, but he was!

Miss Rooke turned up again from Manchester. Dad saw her

again at rehearsals, but nothing could be the same as it was before. He met her with only interest and found her this time too transparently feminine! He had lent her his book on Beamish and reminded her of it, and it was returned by post days later. Had she read it? He rather doubted it, although she swore she had. But the absence of any comment about his work hurt him. He had lost his ardour for her – luckily, maybe. The first night of *The Greatest of These*, the dull, old-fashioned Sidney Gundy play in which she was appearing, prepared him for the fact that was made painfully clear to him: his goddess no longer had a pedestal.

Next play for rehearsals: *Trelawney of the Wells*. Dad was playing a part in this: the supercilious, discontented, jealous, flashy, Ferdinand Gudd. For this part, by the way, his beard had been shaven off. He had grown it out of laziness after not acting for a while, but Elizabeth rather liked it and Dad could not get used to shaving again.

The cold weather was starting again and, as their 'dear' landlady had nothing to give them for warmth on the floor, they wrote to Croydon for anything they could find and were luckily sent some quite useful bits and pieces that soon adorned the floors of their miserable rooms.

For Elizabeth's birthday, my father had made great plans. On Monday morning, at the rehearsal rooms, he found a parcel waiting for him from Thompson, the photographer they had supped with a few nights before. Enclosed was an enlargement of the photograph he had taken at that dinner of Ken lighting a cigar, printed on red paper, with a flame effect. It was very effective and much admired generally. Dad was very glad it had come, for if he could get it framed it would make another present for Elizabeth. Sure enough, framed it was in good time, by the chance of there existing a frame maker who approved strongly of the Repertory theatre.

Elizabeth's Birthday: 31 October, 1911

Elizabeth got up for breakfast on her birthday – a most unusual thing for her – and with the great bowls of coffee (French style) and hot rolls my father had ordered for breakfast, she opened her presents. There was a pair of bedroom slippers and a whalebone hairbrush from Ken, a packet of chocolate from Jon Jon and the framed photo with which she was delighted. Also, there were letters from Muriel and Renee enclosing, much to Elizabeth's delight, £1 and cards from numerous other members of the family.

The next week, Pavlova, the dancer, was advertised to appear at the King's Theatre. She had drawn London to the Palace for several months; along with her, as musical director, was Ken's old friend from the Court days, Theodore Strov! With her also, in a one-act play (which, Ken learned subsequently, was introduced into the programme solely to make it legally a dramatic entertainment), was his old flame Marjorie Day, who had apparently found work at last! My father saw that entertainment on the Monday night when he ought to, by rights, have been either learning his lines or seeing the quadruple bill at the Royalty, but did not feel up to either. All the other seats were full, so he and Elizabeth climbed up to the gallery.

The one-act play was badly acted and Marjorie iniquitous (although with a pretty frock). Some of the concerted dancing interested them and the music was wonderful throughout. But Pavlova did not impress them; her partner was a nonentity with instructions to take applause after each dance well upstage behind her! Pavlova did five tiny dances, or rather the same dance in five different costumes, and did not set the Clyde alight, which, from her attitude at the curtain call, she had obviously anticipated doing. There were several bouquets, which my father felt convinced were carried by the crew from town to town!

During the next few days, they were busy rehearsing: Macaire must get the fall right, do it time and time again; someone has to be there to fire the gun or shout 'Fire!' But it does not always happen that way...

Tuesday 21 November began the rehearsals proper. My father had been a little terrified at the casting of Ben Field, their low comedian, for Bertrand – an excellent part – which he felt might easily kill *Macaire*. But no, at the rehearsal it transpired that nothing could kill *Macaire* and that Field was not going to clown and overplay as he had feared. On the contrary, he was excellent in the part.

My father was still very busy indeed that week, as you can imagine, still learning words and fitting on clothes and finding the personal properties attendant on the part. On Saturday 25 November, there was the final dress rehearsal attended by Mrs W G Henley, who declared him better than Titheradge or Tree, the only other actors who had played the part. There was a little, not uninteresting, scrape with Caplin during one of those last rehearsals: he, so all the rest of the cast had taken care to inform him, had gone quite beyond himself during the season, insulted people right and left as a matter of course and had made himself so unpopular with the entire staff that there were frequent threats to 'do for him', etc. There was an air of discontent about the theatre and notices were being given in every few minutes. Well, so far Dad had not, except in Trelawney, been produced by him, until *Macaire*, where, because he had produced himself, it had not come to loggerheads!

It was at that time that the moment for his death arrived, but there were no soldiers present to shoot him, so he heard the word 'Bang!' pronounced verbally by Caplin from the stalls. He fell with relief, before, to his amazement, he heard himself called a fool, told to get up and was asked why the devil he had fallen. At which piece of his pleasantry my father refused to rehearse any more that night or until the proper people were there to rehearse with. He left the stage to change; he had to go to some trouble to make it quite clear that he was cutting Caplin from the remainder of the rehearsals, and he arrived at the dress rehearsal the next day looking for trouble – but none arrived. Caplin apologised before the rehearsal for his bad manners, so it was silenced.

Kenelm Foss's notes on Macaire

Monday 27 November

The first night of *Macaire* was one of the best days of my father's life. There were no intervals between the acts ('glory be'), which made the whole thing even more of a one-man virtuoso show. He thought he did not catch on in his first scene, but as soon as he started picking pockets he had them, and after a wild fantastic dance with a fiddle by him there was a round of applause. In the second act all his points went in a way that was unmistakable, and it did not need the fall of that second-act curtain to know that even without the third act (his best!) he was a success! (He ate grapes, by the by, hurriedly in each short interval.) The third act went perfectly; he had worked the thing up to the tremendous end.

He was determined that just for once, before he left the stage, he would be a real admitted success. He got to the very end, his villainy was unmasked, he had climbed the stairs, revealed himself as Robert Macaire – only the gunshot remained, but it never came! So, at a loss, he pitched himself down as arranged and died from no known cause. But he knew he had spoiled it. The audience was left wondering, which they ought not to have been, not that he could complain of the applause – it was deafening.

Curtain after curtain, and someone he could only believe was Wareing had arranged a personal call for him alone. It was lovely! He was still upset by the absence of the gun, but it was a really proud moment. He was a success! Just for a minute, just for once! The notices were splendid for the play and for my father, although some papers declared he had committed suicide.

> Mr Foss gave an admirable rendering of the part – portrayed the ragged ruffian with a nice sense of abandon, never overdoing the swaggering side of the character and playing convincingly throughout.
>
> *Glasgow Evening Times*

> Kenelm Foss reveals himself as a very capable actor, meeting all the demands of a very trying part. He put just that soupçon of the burlesque, tragic airs the part required.
>
> *Glasgow News*

The unusual experience was very good for the somewhat dispirited person he was at that period; more of it would have been bad for him. He accepted that applause as a matter of course, and bowed his acknowledgements after the first three nights with languid indifference. Although he had always been fairly popular, his admitted success brought to him more open acknowledgement of the goodwill people bore him, women especially!

This was particularly true of the wife of his friend Percy Marment, a dangerous woman, as he laughingly called her to her face while meaning it with the fullest sense in his heart! The lady was voluptuous, distinctly comely, vulgar and with the soul of a chorus girl, but dangerous! Only one thing could have happened eventually, so far as he could see; he would have been literally seduced and plunged into a hell of a mess, without any satisfaction! He was saved only when they moved, after Percy took another assignment. Dad had to be rude to her more than he had ever been to any other woman. He was so pleased though that his friendship with her husband remained unscathed, but, oh, the relief.

To go back to the reviews, here is another nice one from the *Daily Record* (the Glasgow version of the *Daily Mail*):

> Such a play affords little scope for the majority of the players, who are merely puppets, but it does make demands on the bearer of the chief character. One could wish for no better exponent of it than Kenelm Foss. He is indeed excellent, revealing with point every phrase of the complex character, and the enthusiastic reception he received at the close was thoroughly deserved!

There remained just the evening papers and the *Westminster Gazette*, which was extremely kind to him and ended by saying that he had done much notable work under the Royalty management, but that this was his most memorable achievement. Doltie, the author of the critique in question, told him (and he was a particularly unemotional Aberdonian) that one only saw a performance like his Macaire once in a lifetime!

So this is the point: whether he was good as Macaire or not, for once everyone said he was good, which in the theatre comes to the same thing. Only one more note about *Macaire*: towards the end of the week his part went much better because people were coming back. On Friday there was applause for his entrance, which helped him immensely. He was covered in bruises by the end of the week, owing to him continuously falling down the steps in the same place. And now that is enough about *Macaire*!

Towards the end of the week, Wareing asked my father whether, if some of his friends he had made in Glasgow during his three years there wished to make him a small presentation as a parting present, he should have any objections. Further, if he had no objections, whether a cigarette case containing a small cheque would meet with his approval. Now, I put it to you, what could a man say? My father flushed and stammered of course and muttered something about his being extremely grateful, but felt very awkward and wished even that no such project had been mooted.

His distaste increased when he heard that Barker had been invited to contribute. A printed letter had been sent out – and in connection with that letter, he really did feel rather touched at the news that Ben's printer had insisted on doing it 'gratis' and had weighed in with a prescription as well. Members of the company had contributed, and even some members of the audience, unknown to my father personally, had asked to be allowed to figure in the list.

It was all very flattering and he was not ungrateful, but wished to Heaven it had not all been done – especially Barker! The idea of Barker receiving that printed letter made him shiver.

Another, more trivial embarrassment cropped up in connection with the fund. Wareing showed my father the letter, and in it the words 'cigarette case' were preceded by the adjective 'GOLD'! Gemini! Him with a gold cigarette case! One could only hope it would make him turn over a new leaf as regards clothes!

You Can Never Tell was by this time produced without anything worthy of note in its revival, save that Phyllis Ralph was the best Gloria he had ever seen and that the love scenes were 'man and super manned' by my father. She willed him to come back to her in the third act, and pulled him down for the ultimate embrace. Valentine was played by Marment, who gave a good imitation of Barker, who was the ideal Valentine.

What the Public Wants with Lloyd as the newspaper proprietor was now being rehearsed – my father as St John, the only other member of the cast – so he was pretty busy after the lull before *Macaire*, and it was nearly the end of the season, after which he would be leaving Glasgow for good.

They had arranged to spend Christmas at Croydon and had determined to travel immediately after the last performance on Saturday night. Their stay at Croydon was to last over the New Year, and then, if they found a suitable place to stay, straight on to their holiday, before finding somewhere and settling down in Hampstead. Their own home at last! Please God!

The late morning and afternoon before leaving was spent buying Christmas presents and, after my father's work that night, they packed such gifts as they bought elaborately in white tissue paper and tied with red ribbon, with little doll's labels and absurd sticky little stamps with pictures of Santa Claus on them. It took them till two in the morning, believe it or not, after which they slept in, as they say in Scotland. The next day was Ken's birthday, 13 December.

In the morning, they had breakfast in their dressing gowns – a special breakfast – and then opened presents: a dear little letter from Elizabeth; Arnold Bennett's calendar; a purse and a little gold safety pin from Jon Jon; and a letter from his sister Muriel, enclosing 10/-, to be spent on something he wanted. Books, of course. W H Hudson's *Swan Mansions* and H G Wells' *The Country of the Blind*. It was a very pleasant day and a wonderful meal cooked by Elizabeth for all the friends he had made (if fairly late) since he'd been in Scotland.

Next day, their last day, was rather sad. They finished the packing, with lunch hastily summoned at Thompson's (the photographer's flat). Then they rushed home (accompanied by Combs, who wished to say goodbye to Jon Jon), to hand over the baggage to two of the theatre men who were calling for it. After that, they had some food in the kitchen of the landlady – she had been ill in bed for two days. They were sad to see Ken and Elizabeth leave; they would miss them so much, and Jon Jon – and he them, one would imagine.

Then it was to the theatre for the last performance of *What the Public Wants*, a hasty shampoo over the dressing room basin by his dresser and then round the theatre for the most depressing of all duties: farewells.

Nearly all of those goodbyes were plain sailing. Only one incident stands out. Little Miss Grey, the ingénue who had been a little smitten with my father in the *Macaire* week, brought him an autograph book to sign. In it, nearly all the signatures were underneath quotations from plays. As he was somewhat down in the mouth, having felt seedy for some time, and perhaps a little morbid, hardly thinking, he signed above his name the last line spoken by Macaire, 'Death – What is Death?' He did not, he swears, realise its aptitude to his departure until poor Miss Grey burst into tears and his honest Scottish friend McClune began to snuffle. Wareing and Lloyd and Miss Norman and Armstrong (with flowers for Elizabeth) saw them off at the station. They had, as usual when travelling with Jon Jon, a carriage to themselves – much as he hated Glasgow, it was a mournful business, that last evening.

And so ended that chapter in his life.

Christmas 1911

Christmas at Croydon followed a dreadful journey from Scotland, but there was a very warm welcome from (amazingly enough) all the family, and good food! My father had been on a vegetarian diet, partly through lack of money, but when he saw the pheasants – well! Their little gifts, so beautifully wrapped by Elizabeth, were received with thanks and pleasure. Jon Jon enjoyed it all, having too many gifts from all the family. Numerous relatives popped in on Boxing Day and they all played silly games after lunch, which my father thought were just right for the day, but might have been boring had they carried on too long.

My father actually always liked family get-togethers, present-giving and everything that went with special occasions, and was always brilliant at games and charades, as one can imagine.

All the family felt that Dad should have a holiday before starting to look for work and a permanent home once again. He was hoping to hear from the Stage Society soon. In the meantime, he had been receiving small amounts of cash for odd articles he had written in his spare time, but not enough to live on. My grandmother had asked a doctor to check him over, as everyone was worried about him; he did feel very lethargic and was still spitting blood every now and then. The doctor came and gave him a good check-up, but only said that he was obviously overworked and overtired, and that a good sea holiday should do the trick.

They decided to try Cornwall for their destination; they had numerous relatives dotted around that area who should know somewhere they could rent. He should go first to get the lay of the land. St Mawes, near Falmouth, seemed a nice place, and they had relatives there as well.

Later in the week, Dad, Elizabeth and Jon Jon went to Clapham to see Elizabeth's mother. She was so pleased to see them as usual. She had a huge Christmas tree and 'piles of lovely grub' that was enjoyed by all ('Jon Jon is a poppet and doesn't he know it!' Mrs G would say). She was as worried as everyone else about Ken's health; he was grateful for all the sympathy, and all the good food helped him. He promised to fix up a holiday as soon as possible and, on returning to Croydon, he made a start by booking a train to Falmouth.

Later my father said, 'By the way, I don't think I've mentioned my new blue suit. If I have, it is excusable, for I so rarely have new clothes! And this is made-to-measure too! I used the presentation money from my leaving-Glasgow party (I couldn't have afforded it otherwise), and it seemed to meet with approval, especially with Elizabeth, and of course I have been wearing it all over Christmas.'

My father didn't really want to take a holiday, especially on his own, but he realised that he really needed one and hopefully the sea air would at least help. Regarding his visit to Cornwall, on the day in question he felt keenly that he didn't want to go on the confounded holiday at all! All part of his phase of lassitude, he supposed it all seemed such an effort! But the whole thing was settled and it seemed he had to go, so he went. Dear old Harvey's farewell was to give him half a crown for his lunch on the train. Bill (one of his brothers) accompanied him to the station – his hours of business seeming engagingly elastic – and saw him off at Paddington. His carriage was crowded and, to drown the fumes of his fellow smokers, he over-smoked himself almost sick! Finishing the 'Merrish' book, he found it very disappointing. Lunch was welcome, and then it was on to Exeter. Passing there, he was reminded of an adorably pretty little ingénue model he had once kissed (while at art school) in Exeter. It reminded him of her because, having totally forgotten the kissing incident, he afterwards received a letter from her saying she was in pantomime in Exeter, and couldn't he come down for the weekend or longer?

He passed Plymouth and made a mental note that all places were much of a muchness – then came to Truro and mentally underlined that note! His fellow passengers had alighted at Plymouth, so he slept until he arrived at Falmouth. His instructions were to take a cab to the quay and from there take the ferry to St Mawes, where a furnished cottage was waiting for him (thanks to the relatives). It was his only means of getting there, but, to his delight, he was told by a kindly-looking porter that, by the time he got to the quay, the last ferry would have left, which meant that he would have to stay at a local hotel for the night.

So he left all his bits, including his handcase, in the cloakroom, and took his travelling rug to look for somewhere not too vile for the small sum he could run to. He hunted high and low for a decent-looking pub or boarding house to no avail, until at the last minute, when all else had failed, he suddenly found a good pull-up for Carmen and much enjoyed an excellent meal. And with this, the first piece of good fortune, he stumbled on the second with a really good bookshop, where he purchased a book for which he had been looking for some time, *Jomo Bungay*, for seven pence!

He eventually found a melancholy building called the Globe Hotel, where he was shown to his bedroom by a not-too-unattractive female, afterwards being escorted to the common room, where he sat for most of the evening writing to Elizabeth and reading his *Jomo Bungay* with difficulty by the dim light of a broken mantel, by a table covered in old magazines and out-of-date timetables.

He needed a shave, so decided to look for a barber's. He found one, not very clean looking, but efficient enough. He then returned to the hotel and drank two sloe gins with the landlord (an amiable soul) – one at his own expense – and then returned to his bedroom and *Jomo Bungay* at 8.45 p.m.

New Year's Eve, 1911

My father woke to the sound of lapping waves and a lovely view of sea and shipping. After breakfast, which was distinctly good, he went to collect his luggage from the station cloakroom, including his bicycle, Jon Jon's cart and his cases. He found a fellow with a vehicle to carry all these things to the quay for him and to put them all on to the little boat that would take him to St Mawes. The man thoroughly earned his two bob tip!

St Mawes looked disappointing at first sight, but, as they approached it, improved distinctly. The porter at St Mawes undercharged him for the job. Ken was so pleased to find such an honest fellow he recompensed him forthwith.

The cottage had a really magnificent view straight out to sea. Elizabeth had provided him with hot milk in his thermos and some of Harvey's 'annual' cake from Wales to demolish on his train journey, but of course he had forgotten them both. However, they came in very useful just then, the milk still piping hot even after twenty-eight hours' wait. He guzzled them with relish before unpacking.

Shortly after arriving, the Rev. Steven Penny (a distant cousin) popped in to see him (a cheery but dull old soul) and introduced him to a most obliging general store stocked with almost everything one required and undertaking to provide anything they didn't stock from Falmouth. Having placed with them an order 'as long as your arm', he accepted the Reverend's invitation to lunch with him in his rooms. The lunch consisted of cold ham and pickles, and very welcome it was too! Reverend Penny told Ken that he was spiritually in charge of three hamlets, of which St Mawes was one.

My father was at last realising that he was feeling better. The sea air was obviously doing the trick and the fact that Elizabeth and Jon Jon would be joining him in the next day or two must have had something to do with it.

The Cornish air must indeed have been doing him good, for he started singing and whistling and feeling in a boyish mood walking back to the cottage. Arriving back, he finished the day happily in the small room facing the sea, which he had chosen as his writing room. He cooked himself some eggs, drank cocoa and settled down to write. He wrote and wrote and wrote, catching up on all his journals and diary, made a long list of all the books he had read during 1911, and finished reading *Jomo Bungay*. And so ended 1911.

New Year's Day, 1912

Monday 1 January began as picturesquely as ever a romantic could wish. My father rose grudgingly by candlelight at the call of the alarm clock, made a hasty toilette and marched overcoated, for the first time since his arrival, out into the dark and cold. He was greeted by the hoarse toot of the steam tug that he had to catch to Falmouth pier to meet Elizabeth and Jon Jon, who had been travelling all night. They would arrive in Falmouth soon after seven o'clock that morning. A scurry in the dark down the only street brought him panting to the pier.

There they were, Elizabeth and Jon Jon. Elizabeth looked tired and Jon exceedingly grubby! They had had to change at Truro – in the middle of the night, if you please! They had not known this as they got on the train at Paddington, and it was rather a shock for poor Elizabeth. Her mother tipped the guard to wake her in good time, which he did by rushing into her compartment as the train steamed into the station, telling her that the Falmouth train was on a different platform and already getting up steam! It was a dreadful rush, but they managed to make it in time.

They found the ferry rather fun, as they had to be rowed to St Mawes just as my father had been when he arrived the week before. He had arranged for the 'lady what does' at the cottage to have breakfast ready for them when they got back. Of course, there was no breakfast waiting, so Elizabeth had to prepare it while he and Jon just got in the way. It was rather nice though; the sun decided to shine on them that morning. A Happy New Year's Day!

They spent the first morning on the beach, Jon Jon loving it but my parents (to be) deciding sadly that the sea is never so wonderful as when one is young. Elizabeth collected pretty stones and shells in a bucket, Jon Jon covering them with his own interpretation of prettiness! Elizabeth, of course, was *my* mother too, but I wasn't born until 1918 and a lot was to happen before then in my father's career. Wrapping presents prettily and collecting shells from the beach were things I remember we did later with her, as she had done with my brother Jon at St Mawes.

My father was still undecided about what to do with himself work-wise, when, on arriving back at the cottage, something arrived out of the blue, as it always seemed to: they found a wire from the Stage Society. Would Ken come as soon as possible to produce a play for them? *Rutherford and Son*. What was as soon as possible?

Dad wired back: 'Straight away not possible – maybe ten days time if OK – please send scripts, etc.' Elizabeth added, 'And cheque.' They discussed it that night and decided to go. My father would make up his mind completely about his future when they got back to London. They waited a worrying few days for a reply, but eventually the scripts and cheque arrived, so they were all set for a return to London.

Later, another pleasant week by the sea, they packed and were ready to leave. My father realised that he had never once used his bicycle after all the trouble of bringing it with him! Before they went, they had a nice send-off lunch with the amiable Pennys ('what a nice couple'). They travelled back to London – not so nice for an eighteen-month-old boy. The train took six or seven hours, with not much entertainment for Jon except looking out of the window, or sitting on the floor grizzling! He was a complete pest the whole journey! Halfway through the morning they managed to give him a bottle to try and soothe him in the hope that he might drop off to sleep for a while, but no such luck! They put him in the luggage rack, thinking he might be amused for a while, but he just sat bolt upright and pulled the alarm cord, so a hasty retreat from there was needed!

Eventually, they arrived at Paddington. Jon Jon was bright as a button, my parents shattered, but it was wonderful to see lovely old London again. They went to Croydon for a while before deciding what to do. Obviously, one of the first priorities was to find a permanent home, preferably in Hampstead. My father was feeling much more himself and was hoping that this could be a new start for him in the theatre.

Next day he went to The Court to see what was going on

regarding *Rutherford and Son*. Not much, it seemed! Nearly all the cast was acting in other plays and so would not be available until early evenings. He left a large notice on the board in the rehearsal room stating that he would be there the next evening and hoped the cast would be there too. It did at least give him the daytime to look for prospective flats to let.

The next day, Tuesday 16 January, Dad met with Miss Sowerby, the authoress of the play he was to produce, and found her to be a nice, sensitive, clever and remarkably non-arty young English lady – a very odd person indeed to have written that grim, dour, but rather interesting play. He found her living with her friend, a Miss Morgan, in a pleasant tiny house in Cheyne Row, where they spent the whole morning discussing the play.

But there were many problems ahead. It was during these discussions that he learnt about the cast. Oh dear, McKinnel, who Dad had met before when he was doing 'walk-ons' at The Court, thought he was God Almighty according to Dad, and he was not keen on taking instruction from him as producer. 'So impervious to reason, such a pig!' My father did find a way of dealing with him eventually, by applying humour, but it was very weary work. Then there was Homewood, who my father knew would be appalling, and was. Miss Morgan, the author's friend, was artificial and not a bit like the part, and Blakeiston, who was playing the curate's son, attempted to be funny all through the play because, as he said to my father, 'After all, I am playing a clergyman.'

My poor father had trouble with the scenery. He knew what he wanted: decent wallpaper and furniture! Surely that was not too much to ask? But the 'drunken, incompetent little manager' tried to palm him off with an oak chamber and benches! It was a bit of a trial, that play, but he had to take it philosophically as a moneymaking concern – after all, he had accepted the twenty pounds offered – or life really would have been too hideous.

Poor Dad, scenery was his speciality! He couldn't really concentrate unless that was right, and not caring for any of the cast didn't help. Ah well, one never knows!

They rehearsed and rehearsed the cast whenever they could get everyone together at the same time. They were behind schedule, but he carried on and eventually the first night was upon them. Unfortunately, due to the various obstacles put in his way, my father's interest in the whole thing had waned, but the first night came and at the performance everything miraculously fell into place. Certain blemishes apart, and although the play when played was not as good as when read, it was a fair performance.

Unbelievably, it became an amazing success; the newspapers were enthusiastic, with interviewers spilling their superlatives all over the shop. The public flooded in and filled the theatre every night. That no one recognised his existence bothered Ken not at all. As he had said before, he had merely taken the job for the money when he and Elizabeth were in dire straits, so his money was earned and that was sufficient.

My father and mother soon moved back at Elizabeth's mother's at Clapham, realising it would be more convenient both for rehearsals and for looking for a home. Mrs G was over the moon to see them again, and they her. There was a friendlier atmosphere than in Croydon, although Harvey would miss having Jon Jon around. After the first night of *Rutherford and Son* and its success, my father thought he must have had something to do with it! There was a lull in the work after that, but Dad was glad of the rest after such a trying time.

Pleasant as it was in Clapham, they needed to find somewhere else to live, especially as Mrs G had said they too were looking for somewhere larger, as her son, Tom, Elizabeth's brother who lived there, had now married and had a child. Also, Jon Jon was now older and needed somewhere to run around, hopefully a garden. Out of the blue, again, my father was offered a small part in a play called *Shades of Night*. It was a very small part, but better than nothing and a great help money-wise as usual. Then, believe it or not, they found a flat in Hampstead where they so desperately wanted to live. A friend of a friend heard of a place that was going at Heath House, so they rushed round to have a look.

It was a lovely old house, but strangely built with lots of corridors and stairs. Elizabeth liked it; she thought it had plenty of character. The flat in question belonged to, or at least was being leased by, Oliver Onions, the novelist. It was pretty near perfect, so that was one problem solved.

The next week, on 28 January, my father was in town and popped into the *Daily News* office for any luck regarding articles or whatever. It was mentioned in passing that Galsworthy's play *The Pigeon* was in its last four performances, so, as he had always wanted to see it, he resolved to go that night and incidentally see his friend Eddie Lloyd who was appearing in it and talk about Wareing's long silence. He was going to sit in the pit, but he got talking to someone he knew ever-so-slightly who said to him, 'Come with me up to the dress circle,' just as he was about to sit down next to a fair-haired and freckled young man who asked if he was Mr Foss.

Dad noted of the meeting:

Lo and behold, it was an old chum from school days: Ben Travers. We reminisced for a while. He was something in John Lane's publishing firm, and considering how long it was since we last met, we got on not too badly. I must certainly keep in touch with him. As for the entertainment, I enjoyed the first little piece, *The Constant Lover*, most amusing and well-acted by Eddie Lloyd and a charming, most kissable Gladys Cooper. *The Pigeon* requires a little more thought bestowed upon it in criticism – I think I would like to read it first, before seeing it again.

My father was indeed pleased to see Ben Travers and kept in touch with him as he said he would, Travers eventually made quite a name for himself in the theatrical world and wrote many successful plays.

The next day my father found out that Wareing was in town, so he was hoping to see him regarding the money that was collected for him when he left Glasgow, which had not been received or mentioned – at least not all of it. Odd cheques had arrived here and there, with promises of more to follow. Ken wondered why. Probably some people had promised money but actually never paid it in. He had also been told that some letters addressed to him had gone astray, due probably to their numerous moves. Even so, some of that money would have been pretty useful then.

The post was a little late that morning, but when it arrived he recognised Wareing's handwriting on one of the envelopes. He tore it open in anticipation and read, 'Please meet us in the bar of the Savage Club at twelve noon today', 'us' meaning Wareing and Granville Barker! He told Elizabeth about the letter and they were both intrigued. Naturally, he rushed there post haste, and there they were! He was so pleased to see them – the two gentlemen who had been instrumental in helping him in all his early days as a struggling actor and play producer. They had both taught him so much.

They shook hands and, after ordering drinks, Wareing said how sorry he was that they had not been in touch for so long, but they had been arranging something that they hoped he would like the idea of. He went on to say that it had been suggested by many people that my father should go into stage management. The delay had been in finding the right venue, which was now available; backing had also been found.

Dad couldn't believe what he was hearing! It was hard to take in, but of course he accepted straight away. This was a wonderful opportunity, and he took it with open arms. The venue was the Little Theatre in the Strand, in the West End. Wareing also said that they hoped that he would try, by hook or by crook, to induce G K Chesterton (who was all the rage at the time) to write a play for him to produce for the inauguration of that theatre. It took my father nearly eight months to achieve this – but more of that later. He asked when he could start – 'As soon as you like' was the reply.

Talking to Elizabeth that night, he said that all the worrying and indecision was now over. He just could not believe that this wonderful opportunity had happened to him. He had already promised to play a part in *Beamish* for a French production in Paris the following weekend, so they decided to go to Paris for three days, leaving Jon Jon with Elizabeth's mother. His French was very good, so there was not much of a problem learning his words for the part. Afterwards they would return to London to start another phase in Dad's life, 1912.

1912–1913

It later came to my father's knowledge that a Miss Helen Brown of the Glasgow Repertory Theatre Company actually suggested that he should go into theatre management, and it was Hugh Robinson who suggested that he should persuade G K Chesterton to write a play. My father was naturally very grateful to both of them.

My father had started to write a play himself, *The Average Man*, which he was quite pleased with. He continued to write this after he had settled into 'The Little' and got the lay of the land. He managed, eventually, to get an interview with Chesterton, but getting him to write a play was to prove a lengthy business. There was the interview, the talks and all the travelling to and from Beaconsfield where Chesterton lived. My father didn't drive or even own a car. He had to make the long journey by train, sometimes only to be rebuffed if the timing wasn't suitable or if Chesterton wasn't in the right frame of mind or was busy writing a book. It needed a lot of patience on my father's part, but luckily he had plenty of that.

Dad wrote:

> In October, a brief return to the stage, in a part most unsuited to my physical fitness, but at least led to my becoming a Brother Savage, which I greatly appreciated. The Savage Club, for actors and members of the theatrical profession, a most coveted award to receive.

When he received the offer of managing 'The Little', he was actually rehearsing the production of Shaw's *Mrs Warren's Profession* for the stage society, to be presented by Alfred Wareing at the Glasgow Repertory Theatre for one week. He had left Glasgow, but occasionally was asked back to produce odd plays. Now everyone seemed to want him, as always happens – nothing at all and then umpteen offers. So he was actually very busy at that time, but did say he would try to get in touch with Chesterton as soon as he could.

Dad also had offers to write articles for several magazines, so things were quite busy for a while. The *Grand* magazine accepted one of his stories, 'The Vicar's Mite' and printed it in February 1912. The *Pall Mall* magazine also printed 'A Present from Home'. During that time he received the following letter from Granville Barker:

> Kingsway Theatre
>
> Dear Foss,
>
> Would you like to do a little journalistic work in connection with some Shakespeare productions I am going to do? Not much to do, not much to get for it. But would you like it?
>
> Yours,
>
> H G Barker

Dad wrote:

> This resulted, middle of June, in my becoming connected with the Press Agency run by one James de Conley at the Waldorf Hotel. For months I only did Barker work and then, mid-August, made an arrangement by which my afternoons only became de Conley's at a fixed salary, which early in October he raised by one-and-a-half, increasing my work proportionately.

About this time, my father tried to get in touch with Chesterton to make an appointment to see him regarding a play. Chesterton was, as usual, very vague, but thought he should be available very shortly. That sounded more hopeful, so my father thought he would try again in a few weeks.

In the course of his press work, my father took to writing rather more elaborate magazine articles; character studies of the famous actress Lillian McCarthy and Henry Ainley. Also, rather differently, Selfridges' 'phone girls', where he met Gordon Selfridge and Vere Smith, editor of *Lady's Realm*, who afterwards accepted several of his stories.

Early in 1913, perhaps the most eventful year of his life so far, my father was still working for de Conley. He was asked to handle and present *Der Rosenkavalier* and the Russian Ballet season for Sir Thomas Beecham. Another night he presented Nijinsky and Karasavina in a novelty dance act at Covent Garden. This was a new role for the ballet stars, but was enthusiastically received.

Dad later received a note from Chesterton saying that he might be able to spare half an hour for an interview some time that week; it was a start anyway!

Dad wrote:

> Managed to tentatively fix a meeting with GKC, where I put the proposition to him re writing a play. He was mildly enthusiastic but said he was busy finishing a book or whatever at the moment, but would let me know as soon as he could.

While Dad had been waiting to find out whether Chesterton would contemplate writing a play, he had been receiving many offers of journalistic jobs that he happily had been accepting! Now he had the time to finish off the play he had personally started writing: *The Average Man*. Wareing had wanted it presented at the Royalty. It was a comedy and was to be staged with another play for a week. It was, of course, the first time it had been seen on any stage.

So here he was – his first play! He was playing the lead and was producing it as well. How's that! He did feel rather elated, to put it mildly. The press was flattering as well:

> Mr Foss presents a theme which is at once interesting and dramatic with many thoughtful passages and many amusing episodes. The play had a flattering reception.
>
> *Glasgow Evening News*

> A love tale with marked touches that stamped its individuality. The characters are sharply drawn and the play calls for more than the ordinary class of acting. At the close the author had to take a curtain call several times, a compliment quite merited.
>
> *Glasgow Evening Times*

Amazingly, a few days later, he had a message from Chesterton: 'I think I can find you a little time for a chat and a discussion regarding the play. Can you get over here some time next week?' Could he ever? This sounded reasonably positive, so he cancelled everything else likely for the following week and wired Chesterton, waiting cautiously for the word, 'Come!'

Kenelm Foss
About 1925

LITTLE THEATRE
SOLE PROPRIETRESS - GERTRUDE KINGSTON

Under the Management of
KENELM FOSS.

Magic
by
G·K·CHESTERTON

NOVEMBER 7th, 1913

*G K Chesterton wrote Magic especially for Ken, to fantastic reviews!
Eventually presented and acted all over the world*

The Joyous Adventures of ARISTIDE PUJOL
by W. J. LOCKE

"Aristide Pujol at your service"

Kenelm Foss as Aristide Pujol, also directed by him and filmed enitrely in France, 1915

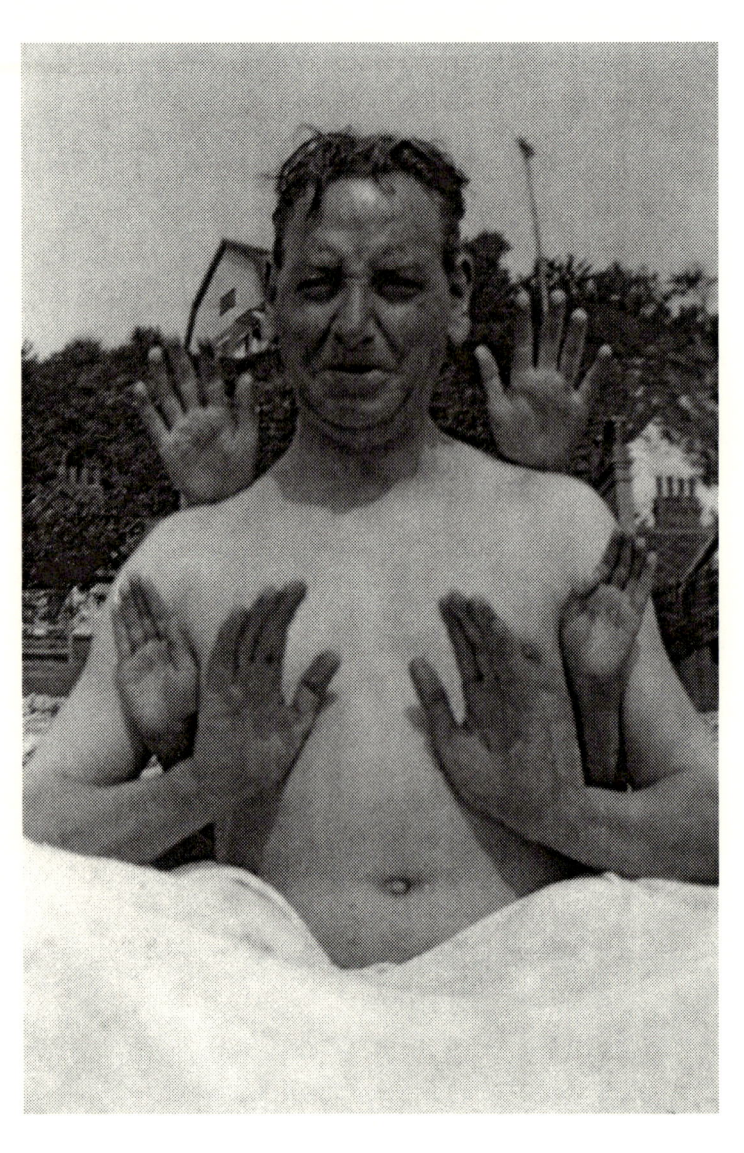

Ken and two daughters' hands, St Margaret's Bay, 1931

Nuncs' Causeway
A Bohemian Fantasy

KENELM FOSS

Kenelm Foss, Actor, Journalist, Scene-Designer, Press-Agent, Poet, Producer of Plays and Films, Novelist, Dramatist and Caricaturist, knows Bohemia as only those can who are in it and of it.

HUMPHREY TOULMIN

Ken's second novel – recieved to much acclaim.
1928

BRITAIN'S BEST " PRODUCER."
—Mr. Kenelm Foss, responsible for
" the Breed of the Treshams," a
triumph of British film production.

Starring Sir John Martin Harvey

A BRITISH PRODUCTION BY ENGLAND'S
LEADING PRODUCER, KENELM FOSS

ASTRA FILMS

Present

CYRIL MAUDE

IN

"The Headmaster"

By Wilfred T. Coleby and Edward Knoblock.
Adapted, designed and produced
by KENELM FOSS

CAST:

Rev. Cuthbert Sanctuary, D.D., Headmaster of Carchester School	CYRIL MAUDE
Portia } his daughters	MARGOT DRAKE
Antigone }	ANN TREVOR
Hon. Cornelia Grantley	MARIE ILLINGTON
Palliser Grantley, her son	MILES MALLESON
Dean of Carchester, her brother	SIR SIMEON STUART
Jack Strahan, Undermaster at Carchester School	LIONELLE HOWARD
Munton, the School Sergeant	WILL CORRIE
Richards Major, Captain of the School	ALAN SELBY
Stuart Minor	GORDON CRAIG
Bella	LOUIE FREEAR

Another hit for Kenelm Foss.
Originally staged at Glasgow Repertory Theatre, now a successful film.
1920

Kenelm Foss Vanity Fair *cartoon, 1914*

"'Alf. Burton' by the Sea."

Kenelm Foss, who played the dual rôle of "Alf. Burton" in the recent Lucky Cat production, "The Double Life of Mr. Alfred Burton," is "somewhere on the East Coast," crouching for his next spring! He was discovered by an indiscreet intruder,

Kenelm Foss by a French Caricaturist.

barefooted, trousers uprolled, asleep in a deck chair a few inches from the salt sea. Part of his face had become hirsute—"K. F." is growing a beard for his lead in "Aristide Pujol," a forthcoming picture which will take him to Paris.

*Kenelm Foss with Sir John Martin-Harvey.
They made numerous films together*

Kenelm Foss with Barbara Everest
Acted together in Aristide Pujol *and as man and wife in*
'Til our Ship Comes In

Group with Kenelm Foss (second from right) and Victor McLaglen (right) sportsman turned film actor

Sir John Martin-Harvey and Kenelm Foss, smoking the pipe of peace between takes of the film Breed of the Treshams

Kenelm Foss
About 1912

Kenelm Foss as Charles Dickens

Kenelm Foss as D'Artagnan

Kenelm Foss plays a hunchback.
A character study from his own film Not Guilty *of which he was the star as well as the author.*

Picadilly Circus held up while Kenelm Foss directs Zena Dare and Mary Odette in a film in 1915

Crowds came at seven thirty on a Sunday morning when Ken thought no one would be about! By quarter to eight the crowds were well into their hundreds.

Kenelm Foss as Edmond Kean

Kenelm Foss with Zena Dare, star of the film No.5 John Street.
About 1915

The crowd stand back while Kenelm Foss directs a film with Lionel Howard and Reneé Mayer, Bournemouth Pier, 1920.

Ken directing Sir John Martin-Harvey and extras in The Breed of the Treshams

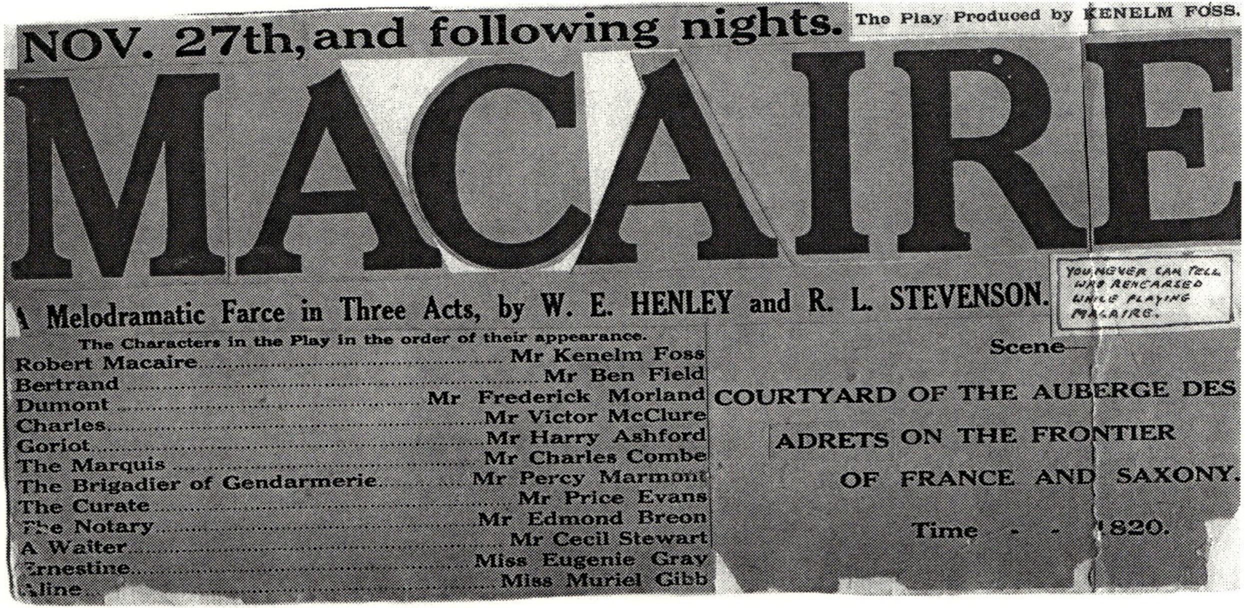

NOV. 27th, and following nights.

The Play Produced by KENELM FOSS.

MACAIRE

YOU NEVER CAN TELL HAS REHEARSED WHILE PLAYING MACAIRE!

A Melodramatic Farce in Three Acts, by W. E. HENLEY and R. L. STEVENSON.

The Characters in the Play in the order of their appearance.

Robert Macaire .... Mr Kenelm Foss
Bertrand .... Mr Ben Field
Dumont .... Mr Frederick Morland
Charles .... Mr Victor McClure
Goriot .... Mr Harry Ashford
The Marquis .... Mr Charles Combe
The Brigadier of Gendarmerie ... Mr Percy Marmont
The Curate .... Mr Price Evans
The Notary .... Mr Edmond Breon
A Waiter .... Mr Cecil Stewart
Ernestine .... Miss Eugenie Gray
Aline .... Miss Muriel Gibb

Scene — COURTYARD OF THE AUBERGE DES ADRETS ON THE FRONTIER OF FRANCE AND SAXONY.

Time — 1820.

Kenelm Foss' first acting role at the Glasgow Repertory Theatre. It was a great success.
Early 1912

*Interior of Sandy's,
a celebrity's bar with signed pictures of stars on the walls
1928*

The Weekly Telegraph, February 9, 1929.

MY MINIATURE MUSEUM.

"Sandy" in his Oxenden Street bar, Haymarket. Note drawings by famous artists on the walls.

Mr. Kenelm Foss, otherwise "Sandy."

NUNCS' CAUSEWAY

¤ ¤

Disagreeing with Mr. Chesterton's dog Quoodle, who said of human beings that 'they hadn't got no noses,' Mr. Kenelm Foss has invented a Club for Noses—or, in Bohemian parlance—Nuncs.

King-Nunc, Hook-Nunc, Snub-Nunc, Skew-Nunc, Blob-Nunc, Dook-Nunc, Beak-Nunc and Quid-Nunc are eight members of the Nuncs' Club, for which the qualifications are poverty and failure, two ingredients which do not always make for unhappiness in the Bohemia Mr. Foss knows so well.

Nuncs' Causeway is rightly called a Bohemian Fantasy.

Mr. Foss description of young life's willing sacrifice to Love is charmingly told, and the loyal Nuncs, sticking together through thick and thin, championing each other's causes, applauding each other success, condoling with each other's failures, give one a true and vivid impression of the real camaraderie existing among the Bohemians of all time.

¤ ¤

HUMPHREY TOULMIN
at The Cayme Press Limited
21 Soho Square, London, W.1

Ken's very popular second novel, 1928

Ken filming a long shot on top of a cricket pavilion

ZENA DARE
IN
"No. 5, JOHN STREET"
By RICHARD WHITEING.

Adapted, Designed and Produced
by KENELM FOSS

A Cold and Frosty Morning.

Filmed in Picadilly Circus

*Kenelm Foss and camera staff directing long shots on location.
Lots of interested fans*

On exteriors at Hastings with the Thompson British production of All Roads Lead to Calvary by Jerome K Jerome. From right to left : John Parker (cameraman), Kenelm Foss (director), Bertram Burleigh (leading man), H W Thompson and H J Ducre (cashier)

Sandy's, No. 25 Oxendon Street, the original Sandy's, became too small to accomodate all its patrons so Ken took over No. 27 which was luckily available. Note the delivery van on the left.
1927–28

Press-notices of "THE AVERAGE MAN"

GLASGOW EVENING NEWS.

"Mr Foss presents a theme which is at once interesting and dramatic, with many thoughtful passages and many amusing episodes. The reception last night was most cordial.

GLASGOW HERALD.

"'THE AVERAGE MAN' is essentially a drama of dramatic contrasts. Mr Foss has drawn two types of men and two types of women. The play had a flattering reception.

GLASGOW EVENING TIMES.

"A love tale...with marked touches that brought it out of the rut and stamped its individuality. The characters are sharply drawn and the play calls for more than the ordinary class of acting. At the close the author had to take a "curtain" several times -- a compliment quite merited."

WESTMINSTER GAZETTE.

"A very attractive comedy with thoroughly sound work in characterisation and a great deal of sympathy in the development of the plot. It is, like "THE PIGEON", a play with a real understanding of the misfits, though Mr Foss draws a more practical moral.

Kenelm Foss played the leading roll as well as directing and producing this play, 1913

Exterior and interior designed by Ken and his brother in law Tom Gilson. Much Admired! Sandyman stolen but happily returned later

With Bernard Shaw's compliments

✗ Sorry I couldn't come: my work of late has only
called at bedtime. Always send one two tickets when you send
any: I am a married man. I enclose a subscription humble your
first review.

10 Adelphi Terrace, W.C.
16/1/09.

Bernard Shaw's message to Kenelm Foss

A Modern Miracle of Catering

HE's a deuce of a chap—this Sandy-fellow! Born just Kenelm Foss, he was not content with being a recognised power as a novelist, poet, journalist, dramatist, scene-designer, actor, and producer of plays and films, but six short years ago he must needs butt into the catering-business as well.

And when "Sandy" Foss butts into anything, he butts with some result! Almost as soon as he opened his now famous sandwich-bar, beside the Prince of Wales Theatre, it became a huge success. Starting off on his own on a gross capital of less than £50, Foss was, to commence with, his own buyer, cook, cutter, and sole barman—to say nothing of charwoman and sink-boy! If you want a thing well done you must do it yourself, 'tis said; and Foss *did*. Famous artists, friends of his, admiring his enterprise and grit, rallied round him, and not only patronised him and insisted on their influential friends doing likewise, but presented the new rendezvous with roiginal pictures, *drawn on the actual oak panels of the shop*, complete with friendly inscriptions.

Soon, the walls proudly exhibited authentic and valuable works by, among others, Sir William Orpen, John Hassall, Brainsfather, a Bonzo by G.E. Studdy, George Whitelaw, Bert Thomas, Alfred Leete, and two other *Punch* artists, L. G. Stampa and George Morrow.

Later were added fine examples of the art of Joseph Simpson and the great James Pryde.

Sandy's speedily became the daily meeting-place of celebrated Bohemians of all kinds—actors, musicians, painters, composers, dramatists, novelists, critics, journalists.

Article and cartoon from Good Cheer, December 1930

A KENELM FOSS COMEDY.

The Ideal are putting out English one-reel comedies, including Kenelm Foss' much-admired production, *Till My Ship Comes Home.* This tells the story of a doctor and his family, who always lived in the hope that fortune would smile upon them some day. It is based upon the well known book by Kenelm Foss, who has been described as "The New Dickens."

* * *

Cinema Chat Sept 15: 1919

Sometimes even the reporters get it wrong. The production was actually called Till our Ship Comes In.

NEW ROLE: ACTOR OPENS A SANDWICH BAR

Kenelm Foss, the actor, behind the counter of Sandy's Sandwich Bar, which he has opened in Oxendon-street, Haymarket, as told by Mr. London yesterday. Enjoying a cooling drink is Herbert Mundin, of "Charlot's Revue" fame.

Theatrical friends enjoying refreshment in Kenelm's sandwich bar.
The 'in' place

THE STORY OF SANDY'S

BEING THE PLAIN TALE OF AN ALL-BRITISH SANDWICH-BAR

As told in the Columns of the

Evening News, Daily Express, Daily News, Star, Daily Chronicle, Sphere, Weekly Dispatch, Daily Graphic, Sunday Express, Passing Show, Sporting Times, Glasgow Bulletin and Scots Pictorial, Western Mail, Tit-Bits, Home Notes, and New York Herald Tribune.

PUBLISHED BY

SANDY'S SANDWICHES LIMITED.

REGISTERED TRADE MARK.

25, OXENDON STREET, HAYMARKET,
AND
65, FLEET STREET, EC,
LONDON.

Front of a booklet which contains quotes from the press and sandwich menu

> You cannot fail to recognise a
> ## SANDY'S DELIVERY VAN
> as it passes on its way to distribute, in City or West-End, our
> 1/6, 2/- & 2/6 Sent-out Selections. Freshly-Cut; Neatly-Packed;
> Delivery Punctual, Prompt and Free.
>
> See Special Leaflet for Sent-out Menus
> then 'Phone Central, 5954 or 5955.

Sandy's original delivery van. Very attractive and noticable but became too small for the enormous demand for sandwich delivery quite soon after Sandy's opened

Three cuties and a chaperone waiting their turn at the bar with Kenelm Foss in the background on the blower

Magic

Kenelm Foss was the original producer of *Magic*, Chesterton's initial effort as a dramatist, the play being especially written by him for my father to inaugurate his first term of management of the Little Theatre in the Strand.

Although at the end of 1912 my father was still only in his twenties, he had for more than two years been principal producer at the Glasgow Repertory Theatre, staging there week by week plays by Shakespeare, Ibsen, Shaw, Barrie, Arnold Bennett, R L Stevenson, Granville Barker, Laurence Housman, Pinero, Galsworthy, Masefield, etc. In London he was also recognised as a 'highbrow' producer, thanks to his success as a director of *Rutherford and Son* and various ambitious plays for the Stage Society, including Chekhov's *The Cherry Orchard* – its very first presentation in England.

Early in 1913, while producing Shaw's *Mrs Warren's Profession*, it was suggested he should go into management and backing was offered. Only a week or two later, the possibility arose of inducing G K Chesterton to write a play. The actual dragging it out of him was by no means as simple as all that, the labour of doing so extending over eight long months of patience and pertinacity.

To begin with, Chesterton – whose Johnsonian bulk, flowing cape and broad-brimmed black hat had been a familiar sight to my father in Fleet Street – lived in Beaconsfield, Buckinghamshire and, being the most voluminous of writers and therefore the busiest of men, was correspondingly difficult to pin down at any spare moment. Moreover, he didn't particularly want to write a play! He manifested a certain enthusiasm in visualising the completed work staged, but was so perpetually snowed under with new commissions, each one irresistible, that for so long it seemed impossible that his and my father's dream would ever take tangible form.

A genius with boundless energy, quixotically generous and

punctiliously conscientious as regards his comments, Chesterton always struck Ken, on his numerous visits to Beaconsfield, as having little or no system of work. My father also invariably seemed to find this huge person pacing about his medium-sized workroom, dictating in his familiar high-pitched turkey gobble, against time, with a messenger waiting to rush his copy post haste to the printer, as in the case of *Oliver Goldsmith*.

More than once did my father reach 'Over Roads', the house that Chesterton had built himself, to see his over-busy prey observing his arrival and hastily and irritably decamping to some other apartment in the hope that Ken would not have noticed him within (some hope!) and would believe him to be away from home. Mrs Chesterton, incapable of identifying herself with even any social white lies, one time told my father firmly that he had had his journey from London for nothing. But another time, taking pity on him, she it was indeed who – considering with Arnold Bennett that plays, whether lucrative or not, were excellent publicity for the literary artist – was undoubtedly instrumental in getting the play eventually written. That is to say, she helped to get a play written, for what any play turns out to be when finished can be planned by nobody other than the writer.

But much water was to flow under the bridge before anything concrete actually materialised. For literally months, the few interviews my father managed to snatch with the elusive Pimpernel were devoted to eliminating from his mind, tactfully and with all humility, the vision of a gargantuan historical pageant, a fantasy of the scope and size of Hardy's *Dynasts* with hundreds of characters and innumerable scene changes. How good that would have been, but unfortunately completely outside the scope of my father's pencilled capital. He hoped, instead, to obtain an equally authentic and characteristic Chesterton, but taking place in only one scene, or two at the most, and with as few characters as possible – and of those characters, the bulk to be masculine since Chesterton's greatest admirers (of which Dad counted himself one) would not maintain that he ever excelled in the delineation of females.

But always, whenever my father managed to get through to him, did he – huge head and tummy, tiny feet – pace back and forth, talking nineteen to the dozen, bubbling over, literally, with ideas, some good, some not so good, on every subject under the sun with analogies, historical, political, allegorical and literary, punctuated with uproarious laughter at his own generously besprinkled witticisms, some good and some not so good, all interspersed with sneezes, nose-blowing, spluttering and frequent reference to beer and the Almighty. The latter being a veritable King Charles' Head to him, one might feel a mental wreck after one of these meetings! One might regret that it had taken no step nearer one's object, but by Jove, it was never dull! It was characteristic of the man that, though he had striven to evade the interview, each time it had started he seemed quite content that it should go on for ever – until indeed he was soberly reminded by Mrs Chesterton that there was pressing work overdue for completion.

> God built him on a generous plan,
> Because he rather liked the man.
>
> Reginald Arkall

At length, by ruthless pestering, my father contrived to extract from the latest of his utterly confused welter of potential themes the nebulous nucleus of a wild, propagandist, pro-beer farce designed to heap ridicule upon the great teetotaller and Modern Tavern enthusiasts. It was always difficult to talk him out of anything, but in this case as in every other he strenuously tried and eventually got him to see that, if he set upon the motif, it must at least be linked up with some more dramatic and particularly more romantic plot matter! The inevitable answer to this was that my father might rest assured there would be plenty of God in the play, as well as plenty of beer, mysticism, revealed religious faith and what not, in addition to satire, politics, caricature and knockabout humour. A phantasmagoria! A fantasy!

Months elapsed and my father had really begun to despair of transmitting his pipe dream into anything less elusive, when a highly typical letter arrived out of the blue in GKC's own distinctive handwriting, spacing and punctuation:

Dear Foss,

I hope you can forgive the delay in this letter...

I think I could promise a play within a fortnight or less, but not the play I suggested, which was really the dramatisation of a novel I meant to write, and there were two elements in it and the more I think about it the more certain I am that the two stories ought to be separated... I am sure one of them alone would really make a play! For the moment I say no more than that the detachable dramatic part is about hysterical curiosity – a conjuror! But I will let you know shortly with my full scheme, scenario (whatever that is) if you will strain your patience with me, which already I ill deserve, so far as to drop me a line in return to the following points: (1) How much time have I exactly to finish the stuff, before essential rehearsals? (2) If such a play consists of four acts, how long ought each act to last? (3) Will it wreck your chances at all if the sensation turns on the actuality of spirits, ghosts, the supernatural, etc.? I can only ask your pardon once more for this rough statement, but my very haste is a kind of apology. I am in far too much of a hurry to tell anything but the truth.

Yours faithfully,

G K Chesterton

As can be imagined, my father wrote in reply as fully and persuasively as he could, though the date of delivery was still pretty vague, and the practicability of the completed play even more problematic. The general situation was so much more encouraging that it seemed time to make plans for a London season, whether for the near or more distant future.

During the next month or so my father caused a few tactful newspaper paragraphs to be disseminated, renegotiated with a theatre or two for possible dates of tenancy and kept potential backers interested with enthusiastic descriptions of a comedy not yet in existence. But it was all working very much in the dark, and it is easy to guess with what joy he at last received a telegram running thus:

> Rush of work, the Leicester Election! Fear cannot finish play till Sunday; reach you early Monday. Chesterton.

Actually it was forthcoming neither early Monday, late Monday nor early Tuesday! In response to a frantic wire from Dad he got another:

> So sorry about error, whole thing coming tomorrow morning. Chesterton.

That was on 1 July and by midday 4 July silence still reigned! In the afternoon came the following:

> Am sending play today, so sorry for delay which was unavoidable. Chesterton.

And even then it still didn't arrive! My father's Hampstead flat, rented from Oliver Onions and his wife Berta Ruck, was in that great, gaunt, spooky-looking, but by no means unpicturesque building, once a country mansion amidst fields, which figured on the pictorial dust cover of Onions' ghost tale *Widdershins*. Now he really began to wonder whether the place wasn't really haunted and bringing him bad luck.

But believe it or not, it all went well from then on! The Little Theatre that Ken was managing was deemed a suitable venue. The best and most suitable actors were chosen. He and his helpers designed the stage settings, which couldn't have been better – and so to the opening night.

Would it all go according to plan? Everyone prayed, as befitting the play! The theatre was packed and a wonderful atmosphere prevailed. On that first night, Chesterton and my father arranged to share a box with their respective spouses. My mother had not yet met GKC and, before he arrived, Dad bet her a shilling that in his first three sentences the name of the Almighty would occur! At that very moment the door was flung open and the great man, greater than ever in a voluminous evening cape, was shown in by my father's manager, who murmured some trite query as to whether our author often went to the theatre.

'I can't say I do,' boomed GKC, 'and in this, indeed, I have come not so much as a mere member of the audience, as to give myself for the first time the pleasure of seeing my own creations, my own puppets, working at the end of their strings. It is perhaps the only opportunity a man ever gets appreciating the sensations of God!'

Once the final curtain was down, there was no doubt whether the play was a success or not. The audience stood and shouted themselves hoarse until Chesterton – averse to making a speech – was forcibly ballooned on by dad to do so! And then, oh goodness, he thought he'd damned the whole thing by his very first words!

'Ladies and gentlemen,' said he, 'I know that this is a very poor play, if a play at all...' or words to that effect.

My father nearly bit his tongue off with chagrin. He could visualise the critics, unable perhaps to appreciate the play and anxious to get any old peg to hang their cleverness on, repeating: 'Mr Chesterton admits his is not a good play, and we agree with him!' and damning him with faint praise. But Chesterton was not a political controversialist for nothing. That commencement was only his guile. As he warmed to his work, he won the whole audience over so that, as they went out, they were still chuckling at his unexpected addition to the evening's entertainment!

The critics were eulogists in chorus, and soon *Magic* by G K Chesterton became a cult, attracting spiritualists as well as artistes and connoisseurs of literature and humour. There were people who went and saw it twenty times. Algernon Blackwood wrote virtually the whole of one of his books round the atmosphere and emotions it created and suggested, thanks primarily to the enthusiasm of that most discriminating of dramatic critics, S R Littlewood, later to become editor of *The Stage*, and the campaigning he did for the play in the *Daily Chronicle*. This very uncommercial play ran nearly 200 nights in the West End, has been several times revived, played on tour and in rep., on Broadway and the principle cities of the USA, besides being translated into French for the Pitoëff to appear in!

G K Chesterton's play *Magic* was given the whole of the front page of the *Daily Sketch* on Saturday 8 November, 1913. Never has anything like that happened before or since.

After Magic, What Next?

After the 'magical' success of *Magic* things quietened down somewhat for about a month and so it was decided that it would come off on the coming Saturday. Then suddenly things began to pick up again, and this success is generally admitted to be largely down to Kenelm Foss's ability, enthusiasm and untiring energy. My father spoke to a representative of the *Evening Standard* on 19 June, 1914:

> On the Friday morning bookings began suddenly and unexpectedly to leap up, and on the Saturday night we had to turn money away! It was then decided, just before the end of the last act, to run for another week. We did so well that it was decided to keep it on yet another week at least.
>
> *Rutherford and Son* was one of my biggest successes and also a splendid commercial success too; then I have produced in all, five plays for The Stage Society. What I always aim for is, because I firmly believe that it is absolutely essential for the success of any dramatic production, is to make everybody as natural as possible and entirely unstagey, but keep them at the same time full of vitality and to keep the poetic element or atmosphere which must exist if a play such as *Magic* ought in a sense to hypnotise the audience! By the 28th of the month we shall have run a hundred nights! I think that proves my point!
>
> As for me, I started my life as an art student and then my whole theatrical experience has been wholly in connection with the artistic dramatic work studied at The Court theatre, and I think I learned the business under the best possible school of our generation, the Vedrenne-Barker management when they were almost unknown. Afterwards they made me principal producer at the Glasgow Repertory Theatre where I remained for three years.
>
> Then my health broke down and I had to go abroad for a year. I returned to Glasgow to act in and produce my own play, *The Average Man*, while waiting for G K Chesterton to write his play, *Magic* – and so here we are, I can only suppose that by degrees, people have been telling one another how excellent it is. Anyway, it's a success now, and that's all that matters!

1914

The hundredth performance of G K Chesterton's play, *Magic* at the Little Theatre was preceded for the first time by a curtain raiser by George Bernard Shaw, entitled *The Music Cure*, of which the audience seemed to thoroughly approve. When taken on tour, *Geminae*, a one-act play by George Calderon, preceded both plays being produced by my father. Each play was slightly shorter than the normal running time, so they were suitable to be shown together, which proved very popular with the audience, having two plays for the price of one!

The next play to be presented at the 'Little' was one called *Account Rendered*, which was trouble from the start. It was met with derision, and critics panned it straight away. The public were conspicuous by their absence, so my father had to put a notice in the daily papers as such:

> Little Theatre, John Street, WC. May 1st 1914 Kenelm Foss Season. Regarding the play, *Account Rendered*, the play-going public has concurred with the many unfavourable critiques of this play. I have no alternative to accept (although still unconvinced) the general verdict on the play and my production of it. Consequently, it will be replaced on Tuesday the 5th May at 8.45, by a revival of G K Chesterton's play *Magic*, which will be followed on that occasion and at each subsequent performance by Robert Vansittart's *Dusk*, an oriental fantasy to be staged by Kenelm Foss.

My father was very upset with all the adverse publicity for this play, but unfortunately nothing could be done about it. It was most unfortunate when things had been going so well at the 'Little' until then. Owing to the failure of *Account Rendered*, alterations in the programme had to be rushed through. For the working up of the tour of *Magic*, my father arranged an open discussion for one evening in the theatre with G K Chesterton,

Belloc, Shaw, himself and many others, the title being, 'Do Miracles Happen?'

Before becoming ill again, my father presented *The Impulse of a Night* and *The Three Wayfarers* by Thomas Hardy at the Little Theatre. *Account Rendered* plunged Dad into a law case that lasted for many months. World War One broke out, which meant that no one wanted serious plays then, preferring lighter fare such as *Chu Chin Chow* and *A Little Bit of Fluff*. So his promising stage career came to a halt, at least for the time being.

While my father's theatrical life was having its ups and downs and his health troubles didn't help the situation, Elizabeth was carrying on in her usual way, looking after Jon and everything 'backstage' so to speak, always so good at that and never one to panic. Dad's health problem was always there, but they seemed to get round it and other worries in their own way. At least there was more money around, or had been up to then.

At the start of World War One, Dad was, in a word, branded (after his record in Glasgow and the running of the Little Theatre in London on what lowbrows called highbrow lines) with the stigma of an intellectual producer and, as everyone knew, intellectual plays were not what the public wanted just then. Nobody wanted him either, not even Lord Kitchener, Dad having left Glasgow in very poor health with TB. However, money had to be earned, but the advice of a doctor was, 'Find something with a chance of being in fresh air.'

After a period of enforced idleness, things turned up, as they usually did. Quite by chance he met an old friend, Maurice Elvey, the brilliant film director and one-time actor who had made numerous very popular films in the up and coming film industry. Over a drink he said to Dad, 'You're just the sort of person we are looking for. I might have a part for you in one of my films!'

The film business was certainly new to Dad. He had hardly ever been to a cinema or even thought about films in any way, but was this going to be another stage in his life? Could be! He certainly had plenty to offer, with production knowledge and acting and writing skills!

'Come along to the studio and have a look around,' said Elvey. 'I shall be there all day tomorrow.' So a meeting was arranged, just like that! He certainly had more of a spring in his step as he went home to tell Elizabeth. When she heard what he had to say, she felt everything was going to be all right again. It certainly was! And the rest, as they say, is history!

Films at that time were very much in their infancy in Britain: two-reelers, comic strips mostly. It needed more people like Elvey, and now my father, to take it all in hand or at least help. They had a good heart to heart and came up with some great ideas. Theatre actors were feeling the pinch for lack of work and Dad was sure lots of them would jump at the chance of having a go in films. They would have to change their styles of acting a bit, but once an actor, and a good actor, it could be done or fall by the wayside. As all films then were silent, stage actors were all right – it was only when the talkies took over that some would be in trouble. Some voices were not always suitable for sound; not in the early stages anyway.

Of course, America was well advanced in films, but with the right approach Britain would be OK and get in there eventually. Dad certainly had some ideas that would come to the fore soon enough. He started working with Elvey almost at once. They made *Fine Feathers* straight away, Dad learning the ropes very quickly and very soon writing for Elvey and playing in *Mother Love* and *Love in a Wood*, a modern version of *As You Like It*.

He then worked for Frank Miller in four of W W Jacobs' short comedies for London films. He wrote, for Harold Shaw, two original full-length scenarios produced by Elvey. He was kept busy as soon as he joined the crew! It started just a few days after he entered the building. He immediately felt at home and was certainly happier than he had been for quite some time.

About this time, my mother told him she was expecting again. They were pleased, for Jon Jon was nearly four years old and it would be good for him to have a brother or sister. They were still in their flat at Hampstead, so all was well, at least for the time being. Later, Dad started as a freelance scenario writer, and quite soon after he and two other associates started their own company, Lucky Cat Films. Dad, Guy Newell and George Clark soon started making many excellent films. One of these was *I Will*, an original picture play in four parts written by Dad and produced by the author Hubert Herricks.

> Judging by the enthusiasm displayed at the West End cinema when the picture was screened, Lucky Cat Films has gone far towards achieving their object, which is to provide exhibitors with really good comedy dramas.
>
> *I Will*, written, produced and presented by Kenelm Foss, a delightful medley of fanciful comedy and light social satire, this clever film is noticeable for the brilliant comedy acting of Guy Newell. Novelist, dramatist, stage and film producer Foss has the keenest brain in British film shows. He gives as much time and core to writing a film scenario as he does to one of his own novels, every detail is worked out on paper so that when the scripts leave his hands they are ready for immediate production. Lucky Cat Film Company has been founded to provide real English pictures and comedy dramas. We are glad to hear this, more especially, if all its goods are like the premiere production of *I Will*.
>
> *Evening News and Star*

So he wasn't doing too badly with it all in the short time he had made the transition over to the film studios. Take a bow, Ken! He was loving it, he was in his element, and long may it last!

Michael was born on 22 September, 1914. This was their fourth son! Only two now, as the other two had tragically died earlier. My mother said if she had any more children she would like a daughter, but was quite happy having a son to look after. Jon was intrigued, having been the sole form of attention for so long, but all went well.

My father was in his element in his newly found environment, and of course, as was found out very quickly, he had a lot to offer. All the writing and production skills of his stage career were so useful and he was receiving such praise that it was all a bit overwhelming, but very gratifying, and he was taking it all in his stride.

> One of the most versatile men in the film world is Kenelm Foss, he who has written several successful scenarios for almost every leading British studio, produced his own films, adapted and directed screen versions of scores of popular works, and acted, sometimes in triple character parts. He is now engaged in a sturdy fight for all British films. Fresh from the success of *A Little Bit of*

Fluff, he is now showing to the trade at the West End cinema the first British comedy serial, *Till Our Ship Comes In*, written by him and taken from his novel of the same name, published in book form at the same time. It is to be presented in six once a week episodes in which the author plays the lead role of Dr Foster with Barbara Everest playing his wife.

The Stage

Barbara was to become a family friend. She played in numerous films with my father and I remember her as a lovely person. She went to Hollywood eventually; there were always parts for 'older' English ladies, so she was never out of work. Barbara eventually retired to live in Wimbledon village, where I visited her many times before she died.

Till Our Ship Comes In, a lovely light read, did very well at the box office and serials became popular (as they are today as well on television). I have a collection of all my father's many books. His book of poems, *The Dead Pierrot*, was classed as erotic in those bygone days, but I smile when I read it today and consider it to be charmingly saucy, or whatever word one would use nowadays! I was going to use one of my favourite poems he wrote to dedicate this book, but have decided against it, as it is not really suitable. But here it is:

> Wherever dearest you may be,
> I dedicate this book to you,
> I cannot name implicitly,
> (Whoever dearest you may be.)
> Just who will temporarily?
> Be dearest when this book's on view,
> Whatever dearest you may be
> I dedicate this book to you!

Just before starting his Lucky Cat Film company, Dad had done some work for George Loane Tucker in *Arsene Lupin* and from then on wrote all his scripts before he (George) left England for America. One of their last films was entitled *A Man Without A*

Soul, which was shown at the West End cinema in August 1916, written, adapted and produced by my father. Hardly stopping between films, Ken, 'that hustling producer' as they called him, started on *The Wonderful Year*. Based on the novel of the same name by W W Locke, it is set in the Napoleonic era and tells the adventures of a young man and a girl travelling through France on cycles. It depicts the harmonious details of the life of Paris art students. Dad intended to twist it in such a manner as to cement the goodwill between the French people and us. Another of his films to be produced by his newly formed Lucky Cat Film company was *The Double Life of Alfred Burton*. An August 1918 excerpt from the *Sunday Herald* said:

> The film is a splendid production and Mr Foss was excellent as Alfred; British films are certainly showing the way!

Anyone who lives near Deal in Kent will know the treacherous Goodwin Sands. 'How about making a comic film about a cricket match there?' my father said. He thought it would be fun, and so did lots of others, so it was arranged. *Cricket on the Quicksands!* was the apt title. Naturally it had to be done at exactly the right time and with the right weather, along with the right people chosen. They had to be swimmers for one thing and have the right daredevil approach to the whole affair!

So began a game of cricket seven miles out to sea, on the most treacherous quicksands around the south coast – and a dash for the boat at the point when to stay on the sands a moment longer would have meant disaster! This was the exploit performed by Ken and a party of cinema crew and press friends numbering thirteen in all!

Fifty years had elapsed since the sombre dignity of the Goodwins permitted the intrusion of cricket stumps, and then the game was very short-lived. On the present occasion, the hungry sea, jealous even of the small strip of sand left so briefly exposed, put a sudden termination to the match after a little over an hour's play, a period which is believed to constitute a record. The *Gypsy King*, a larger punt fitted with a motor, which proved unequal to the task, was moored off the foreshore at Deal. It towed a smaller boat distinguished by the name of *Little Charlie*, purely for landing purposes.

The first three miles were accomplished without difficulty, everyone aboard in high spirits and looking forward to the adventure that lay ahead. Another three miles and *The Gull* life-ship, that sentinel of the quicksands which had saved many a ship from disaster, hove into view. Here was an opportunity not to be missed, and those on board the *Gypsy King* spent a *'bon quart d'heure'* fraternising with the lonely light-ship crew whose turn of duty consisted of two months on board to every month on shore! The famous lights of 8,000 candlepower were examined and the visitors were photographed high on the rigging.

The small boat landed the enthusiastic cricketers in two instalments, dashing most gallantly through the famous surf and beaching on the narrow strip of sand left comparatively high and dry from the fickle sea. The wickets were hastily pitched, the movie cameras clicked merrily and the game started. The seagulls that had dotted the sands a few moments before beat a hasty retreat at the height of activity.

Embedded in the sand a few hundred yards off was the wreck of a German submarine that came to grief in early 1917, the wreck of the *Montrose* upon which the notorious Dr Crippen was arrested. It could be seen as well as that of another ship, the *Piave*. But all games have their endings and this one proved no exception to the rule, for the sands began to show a significant movement as though surely to take revenge on the intruders. A dash was made for the boat, which came perilously near to swamping in the surf, but the *Gypsy King* was safely reached and *Little Charlie* put back for the second party, the cricket stumps being by this time awash in the sweeping waters and sinking sands. My father and Jack Kirkdale, the studio manager, were the last to leave. When it was seen the overloading would endanger launching, both of them threw themselves into the sea and swam for it! The cameraman took their farewell shots of the disappearing sands and the staggering wicket and so the adventure was as good as over! There is no mention anywhere of the film being shown publicly, but I am sure it must have been rather fun to watch. From what I have read, it appears everyone had a rather enjoyable time.

After a while, my father started a new project; yet again taking his film crew and actors to France to make the film *The Joyous Adventures of Aristide Pujol* by W J Locke. He had to grow a beard for his role in the lead, but he had done this for numerous stage shows years before and it didn't bother him too much. The early scenes were carried out under difficulties at times, as permits had to be shown. Of course, they didn't arrive on time, so nothing was allowed to be filmed until they did! This was very irritating as it was wasting valuable time; also the gendarmes demanded to see passports and every other document under the sun. It took three days for them all to arrive, so a lot of wangling had to be done, filming from one van, which was provided for all their gear, while the performers acted their scenes under the safe ambush of the larger van.

Eventually the permits arrived, so everything was fine. The gendarmes were happy now and many scenes were filmed in the square where they were parked. The gendarmes joined in the situation and were holding up the traffic, but the crowds were good-humoured and cheered with enthusiasm. Dad said afterwards that the best and most realistic scenes were those when half the people didn't realise they were actually acting in the scene! When the film was shown to the press and critics, my father was praised to the skies, both for the film and for his acting:

> Mr Foss's presentation of and acting in the title role of the film comes as near to perfection as has ever been seen on a British screen! The picture represents a rare combination of pathos and humour and the subtitles are really clever. Audiences should find this entirely British film very enjoyable and for once the producer has discovered a really nice looking baby [me]!

After giving birth to yet another boy in 1914, my mother wondered if she would ever have a daughter. So, just to please her, I arrived on 2 November, 1918, and I was named Fanny Burney after my father's ancestor, the famous authoress. I made my one and only appearance in film as the baby in *Aristide Pujol*, and was even mentioned above.

Unfortunately, Dad was let down on the promise of taking over Windsor Film Studios and was left to finish the film on his own. Luckily, thanks to him, it became a huge substantial hit!

After *Aristide Pujol*'s success and the regrettable deal in not acquiring the Windsor Film Studios, my father, always looking for something new, decided to go abroad to sniff out future film locations. First of all he went to South Africa, where he found many interesting places to make a note of. He then went back to France, which had plenty of places to bear in mind, before going on to New York, where he had talks with many top film names, getting ideas and promises regarding negotiations for swapping some star British films for showing in America. One day he met with D W Griffiths and found him friendly and much more approachable than he had expected.

Returning home after a few months away, Dad was rushed straight into numerous new projects awaiting him. First of all, the well-known stage actress, Zena Dare, was to appear in her first film, called *No. 5 John Street* by Richard Whiteing and, of course, adapted, designed and produced by my father. It was going to be something different; it was to be situated and filmed almost entirely out of doors in and around London, especially in Piccadilly Circus, where quite a few crowds would appear.

Dad had no difficulty in obtaining exterior scenes that were to be mostly screened around the statue of Eros and the flower girls who sat there selling their wares. None but the most enterprising would undertake such a task. But Dad always said, 'Nothing ventured, nothing gained!' He had planned to film the scene at 7.30 a.m. on a Sunday morning, when he presumed most people would be at home or in bed still! However, within ten minutes a huge crowd had gathered and the police had to be called before the scene could be completed! My father told me years later how lucky he was to get all the shots completed in such circumstances, and successfully!

After *No. 5 John Street*, Dad took a trip up to Scotland for the first time since he was the chief producer in Alfred Wareing's Repertory Theatre in Glasgow, which has sadly since demised. He was very popular while there, and his two books, a novel titled *Till Our Ship Comes In* and a book of poems, *The Dead Pierrot* (with illustrations by Elizabeth's brother, Tom Gilson, incidentally), had both been published recently and sold well in Scotland;

one of the poems, entitled 'In Campsie Glen', had instantaneous appeal to every Scotsman. Dad had many happy memories of Scotland and was to go on and film there later with Victor McLaglen, the popular film actor.

The next project he took on was a screen adaptation of Sir Philip Gibbs' novel, *The Street of Adventure*, which is the famous story of newspaper life in Fleet Street. There was some controversy when the film first appeared to the trade; the suggestion was made that the book had been altered to please the viewing public. My father was naturally appalled and replied thus:

Sirs,

Having a fairly wide and lengthy experience of film production, this is the first time I have ever ventured to answer any of my critics. But when I am accused of having wilfully distorted and maltreated through my scenario a novel which I appreciate as much as Sir Philip Gibbs' *The Street of Adventure*, my admiration of the novel compels me to point out that, before writing a word of my adaptation, I informed the author of exactly what I proposed to do and modified my plans whenever he had any suggestions to make. Upon completing my scenario and before directing a single scene I submitted it to him, receiving in reply the following letter:

My Dear Foss,

I think your scenario is excellent, it ought to make a first class picture. Very many thanks.

Yours sincerely,

Philip Gibbs

It only remains for me to add that in not one single detail was the production altered from the scenario shown to Philip.

Kenelm Foss

A small piece of interest regarding the film is that Dad hired the contents of the Old Cheshire Cheese in Fleet Street for some of the scenes in his picture. The famous hostelry was closed for a whole day one Saturday and all the pictures, furniture, waiters and even the parrot were transformed into a studio for Dad. This was done because the dining room of the Old Cheshire Cheese is below street level and it would have been impossible to get sufficient light for the film there. Samuel Johnston, whose famous picture was moved with the rest, must have been surprised!

To celebrate the completion of his twelfth production for Mr H W Thompson, the well-known film company owner, my father gave a lunch party at the Trocadero for a number of his press friends following the trade show of *The House of Peril*. After rendering homage to Mr Thompson for the great financial support he had given him (a greater effect than any other capitalist in the world had ever given for film production), Dad said that in the coming year he intended to only make three films. However, each of them would be a great British film.

Dad had just finished producing *The Glad Eye* from the stage farce, first presented at the Criterion theatre. The star of the show, Dorothy Minto, agreed to make the film. The film had been made in France and was called *La Zebie* by Paul Armont. He was so busy and was so much in demand, which was nice, but could he carry on like that indefinitely?

'If there is a bigger hustler in all cinema land than Mr Kenelm Foss, I haven't heard of him,' said a critic from a local evening paper. 'Mr Foss is a dynamo of unceasing energy, working all the time at top speed while at the same time maintaining a very high quality of workmanship. This super-hustler of cinema land is British to the backbone and his films have all been financed by British capital' (i.e. H W Thompson).

Steady on Dad, you can't carry on like this! You don't want to get ill again, do you? Luckily there were some new names coming on to the scene: the Wilcox brothers for a start, Herbert and Charles – they were to make many celebrated films in the early thirties, but at that moment were learning their craft. My father could teach them a lot! Herbert was to marry the actress Anna Neagle, who was to become very well known in many films to come.

'Talkies', as they were known, were the thing coming on the scene – a bit of a worry for all involved, but nothing could stop it! Some actors would fall by the wayside, but that's just life! The thing was, the Americans with all the money they had would be the main worry. The British just couldn't compete with it, so there was trouble ahead – but not just yet!

My father, on his return from America, started on a film with Victor McLaglen (an athlete turned actor who had won quite a few laurels for his acting). It was to be called *McGlusky the Reformer* and many of the scenes were to be filmed in Glasgow and other parts of Scotland. Ken had been finishing off another film entitled *A Romance in Old Baghdad* starring Matherson Lang and Victor McLaglen (again). While in Scotland, my father had hoped to make a short tour of the Trossachs in search of locations for future productions.

After finishing filming *McGlusky*, Dad went post haste into something completely different. The film was called *Cherry Ripe* and was filmed entirely outdoors. It was a charming English story and showed the most exquisite and typical English scenery (taken in and around Dorking, which has wonderful scenery). The film formed a background for a sweet and tender love story, with Mary Odette playing the lead role, but the critics panned it! Dad had no regrets; he thought it was charming and well-acted. You can't please all the people all the time and it did do very well at the box office – that must prove something.

There have been numerous write-ups about my father and his work. Here is one that stands out and one of which I am rather proud:

> A remarkable feat of energy and enterprise has been completed by Kenelm Foss, who does not know what rest is. He has worked at the studio day and night to get his long list of films finished. He has produced twelve films in eighteen months, representing at least 20,000 miles of celluloid and using many, many well-known actors who are all eager to work under his supervision. All financed by Mr H W Thompson, the well-known business man, who set aside £150,000 for that purpose such was his belief in Foss's ability.
>
> Ken says he will now produce and market films under his own name. Mr Foss, who was producing highbrow plays of unusual stamp at the 'Little Theatre' in London ten years ago, is a versatile genius and is now producing a different type of film every time, most of which have an intellectual note rarely seen in British films.
>
> *Daily Express*

So follow that!

What my mother was doing all the time my father was so busy or abroad, I just do not know! I was only about eighteen months old, Mick was about five and Jon Jon would have been ten-and-a-half. Mum was always so caring and never complained, so I suppose she just carried on as best as she could. She did, of course, have her mother and two unmarried sisters to help out when needed, which they had always done and liked doing. I was born in Bushey, Hertfordshire, so I suppose we must have started moving again! After that we moved to Hastings. Why? I really don't know! But the boys ended up both going to school there.

On one of the numerous trips to France for filming purposes, the whole family went along with Dad. We stayed in a place called Rue de Vinseine, where we had a lovely house with a large garden. I was only four years old at the time, so do not really remember much about it. I suppose the boys were on holiday from school. I know there was a zoo near at hand, for we could hear lions roaring quite clearly. One day we went to Paris and walked down the Champs Elysées, so I am told. It was my one and only time, but, sad to say, I cannot remember any of it. I only know we were horribly sick coming and going on the ferry – as were many others – which was quite a usual occurrence on that part of the Channel in those days!

Josephine Foss MBE

My father was one of a very large family, eleven in all. The boys, all six of them, were sent to public schools in their teens, with the girls going to Woodford House School in Croydon at first before being taught at home by personal tutors.

One of the sisters, my Aunt Josephine, was just eighteen months younger than Dad. She was the one I had most affection towards and subsequently most to do with. As a young girl she was a bit of a tomboy; she liked playing (for a young Victorian girl) what were considered boys games such as hockey and cricket. She was very close to all of her brothers and they enjoyed teaching her how to bowl over-arm! She would miss them a lot when they were away at school and more when they left and got married.

Josephine never married. She could never get over the fact that lots of her brothers' friends were killed in the War, when, so young, she would idolise them, as was only natural. She said there were one or two men who wanted to marry her, men who ran rubber plantations, but things never materialised. I sometimes think she was married to her work, but she had no regrets.

Her life conjures up flashes of Somerset Maugham's short stories set in the rubber plantations of Malaya, shades of Neville Shute's *A Town Like Alice* and more than a touch of A J Cronin's *The Keys of the Kingdom* – the novel based on the white missionaries in China.

From an early age, she felt she wanted to go to the Far East, but first she had to gain a little teaching experience. Unfortunately, the early death of her father deprived her of the opportunity of entering one of the universities that had begun to open their doors more widely to women students at that time. Luckily, she had already trained as a Froebel teacher, so was able to take some teaching jobs before deciding to go abroad: first of all at a school in London then on to a tough school in Burnley.

By now she had set her mind on becoming a student at a missionary college in Westminster and had spent six weeks at a hospital in the East End of London, where she not only learnt a great deal about nursing, but also much about the sorrows and unselfishness of the poor. Jo had obtained prestigious qualifications from her tutoring at home, so at the age of twenty-four she felt she was ready and able to set about her proposed journey to the Far East.

Her goal was to do missionary work and so she set off for Russia without a sign of nerves or fuss – none that showed anyhow! She aimed for China to start with and, with a little help from the trans-Siberian railway, she was on her way. The long and arduous journey took her across Russia, including a memorable stop in Moscow where she stayed for a few weeks, then further east on to China where, after a long and adventurous journey that had taken many weeks, she eventually arrived in Peking, where the weather had become extremely hot, especially after the cold of Russia.

In the cool of one evening, the train finally puffed into a great modern-looking station and there in the centre of the platform was a strangely familiar looking sight (a good omen). A large station clock hung proudly, and on it was inscribed: 'Made in Croydon, Surrey, England' – her home town!

Jo stayed in China for five years, teaching and getting herself acclimatised to the countries so foreign to her. She found the experience fascinating, but the plight of Asian females saddened her; little girls were almost taboo and she found them neglected so often. Baby girls were often discarded soon after birth when the parents found them not to be the boy they had hoped for. The locals often thought that baby girls should have their feet bent over backwards and tightly bound to ensure that they stayed small and dainty.

When Jo arrived in Malay, she found things to be just the same. She decided things must be done to change how these girls were treated and to alter their thinking. She had to do something to eradicate such a dreadful state of affairs, but didn't quite know how to start. It was so difficult to change the locals' bigoted minds. But try she must, knowing that this was her vocation. She knew that she must persevere until she succeeded.

Jo found a run-down building to use as her headquarters (later to be known as the shed!) and, unbelievably, many people offered their services to help in any way they could. Jo soon got things going – that had always been her way. Soon after arriving in Pudu, she found a school being run by a Mrs G Brown; she was doing a wonderful job under dreadful conditions and circumstances, was terribly overworked, badly in need of a holiday and some decent rest, and she was desperate for someone to take her place for a while.

Word had got around that there was a 'miracle lady' in town – a certain Miss Foss who had recently arrived in their midst. It wasn't long before Mrs Brown was heading back to England for prolonged leave and Jo was put in charge of the Pudu English School for girls. This was 1926 and from then on her life changed; she had so many ideas and things she would like to do. Luckily enough she was a go-getter: she would decide what needed to be done, then go and do it, most of the time without permission.

It was soon realised within the authorities that what she was planning was the right thing and so permission was granted, grudgingly at first; she set her mind on the general education and well-being of girls, which had quickly become her main aim in life. It wasn't the education she was solely interested in, but their entire outlook for the rest of their lives.

There were so many things for her to do, like organising new classrooms and dormitories for boarders, as so many of the girls lived too far away to come daily. The hygiene needed improving, as did the buildings, playgrounds and roads leading up to the school that were filled with potholes and rubbish. This took many years to accomplish but she won through, mainly through sheer perseverance, determination and guts.

Eventually Pudu English School became well-known worldwide for her amazing achievements. Jo only took brief trips back to England from then on, basing herself in South-East Asia for the rest of her life. She had made a reputation for herself and the school as one of the most energetic and prosperous teachers in Malay.

In 1935, the British government paid their tribute by awarding her the MBE for services to education. Princess Marina, Duchess of Kent, presented her with it while on a tour of the region – a wonderful tribute to an exceptional lady.

While on one of her holidays to England in 1938, she asked me if I'd like to go back with her to Malay, for a holiday and to see her school, of which she was so very proud. For some reason I declined; I suppose I just didn't have the necessary urge at that time. I was happy with my lot: my family and my job as a kennel maid; it was the thought of leaving my dogs that swayed me, I think! Jo understood, I'm happy to report, and my decision proved a good one, for me at least, due to the unfortunate circumstances that were to come. Could I have survived the internment? Many didn't.

It was a long time before we were to see Jo again, so much was to happen, and there was now a lot of tension in the world. World War Two began in 1939, then Japan bombed Pearl Harbor in 1941; soon all hell broke loose!

In Malay they were worried; quick decisions had to be made. Most of the pupils were sent home to their families, boarders included. Jo, some of her pupils and other teachers decided to try and reach Singapore, but were cut off by the Japanese on the way through. They were made to walk back to Pudu in the blazing heat and then interned in the infamous Changi Prison. Thus a whole new chapter in life had begun!

It was a sad day when, soon after some of the hostilities had started, I received a letter I had written to her, returned to me by the post office. It had been unable to be delivered because of internment; we had no news of her for over four years, when finally she and her compatriots were released in 1945. It was only then that we heard, first-hand, how they had fared under dreadful conditions. We learnt that, right from the start, she had decided to get through things no matter what, organised and making the best of any situation. She wanted to comfort everyone else in their hour of need in the years of Changi.

Miss Foss is likely to be remembered for so many things: her courage and ingenuity, along with the many ideas of evading the Japanese policy of keeping husbands and wives completely segregated from each other. One such idea was the rubbish duty! She volunteered for that straight away and found out that next to the dump, through a strong fence, were the men's quarters! She realised this could be a godsend to the married couples who missed their loved ones so much. They organised it so the married women took turns in taking the rubbish out, identifying themselves to their husbands by writing their initials on cardboard and then waving it at their partners, even if only to touch fingers through the wire if lucky. Never, however, would they speak, in case they were caught by the Japanese guards.

The guards paraded the prison every night; every morning and evening there was a roll call and the women were taught to number off and bow in a proper Japanese way. Early on in their imprisonment, Jo volunteered to do ironing for the guards when they were going to meet their girls, as they wanted their shirts and trousers pressed. The other inmates ticked her off, but she said it wasn't officially war work and the guards paid her in food, tea, sugar and, sometimes, even eggs! They hadn't seen eggs for months. So Jo was forgiven and the other inmates realised it made things easier for them – being reasonably friendly to the guards, that is.

Jo also arranged for them to do sewing to pass the time. The Red Cross sent many parcels, full of almost everything and anything. Most were confiscated, of course, and every one was carefully searched. Sometimes large amounts of material were sent, which was very useful: good quality rolls, even silks – and once they unrolled the material to find someone had sewn in a line of aspirins, which were a true wonder as you can imagine.

When they were eventually released in 1945, Josephine weighed barely five stone and had to be carried out on a stretcher by two male nurses. After a longish stint in hospital, she was sent to recuperate in South Africa (where two of her sisters lived), then back to England for a slow but sure recovery. She was lucky in some ways for having lived in Asia for so long; she was used to eating mainly rice, which was their staple diet.

Many people thought that when she had fully recovered from her prison ordeal she would return to Pudu school, but being nearly sixty it wasn't feasible, as she was actually past retirement age by then. But she did return to Malay to do wonderful work in other fields. Her knowledge of so many languages and dialects was invaluable.

On a sentimental journey back to Pudu a few years later, she found that the road next to the school had been named after her! *Jalan Foss* – she took pride in standing next to the sign for a photo session. After doing wonderful work in Malay and the surrounding areas, when she was well enough, she eventually realised that she should come home to lead a more sedate life. She stayed with friends and old colleagues at first, once at Kingston Hill in Surrey, quite near to where we were living at the time.

We saw her quite often after that; she would come to lunch on a Sunday, after which me and my husband Bertie in the summer, along with Linda, my son Brian's wife, would go to watch our village team play cricket, the one sport she still loved. My son was an excellent all-rounder and she would enjoy watching the village team, Claygate, doing so well.

I can remember her caustic remarks if a player dropped a catch or failed to get a wicket. One of the last things I remember her saying to me was how she'd love to go to Lords to watch a test match. To this day, I don't know if she ever did and I often regret that we didn't arrange it for her.

Later Jo acquired a pretty flat in a complex in Priory Road, Hampstead, especially built for people who had worked for the state. She felt the need to still do things; she needed to tax her brain, so she taught English to foreign visitors to this country, ironically mostly Japanese women. 'No bad feelings,' she would say on many an occasion, as they were of a different generation. I visited her there a lot and we would go out for lunch and visit local sights of interest.

Once, on a drive down Baker Street, we noticed the Beatles Emporium, which was a big attraction back in those days. A few years later, when she felt she couldn't cope by herself any more, she accepted a room in an old people's home in Highgate. I visited her every month; she was still as bright as a button, although by now in her mid-nineties. We still went for walks around the houses and to the local parks that she seemed to enjoy – what a truly amazing lady. She had done so much for humanity and education everywhere. We were all so proud of her. Josephine Foss died aged ninety-six on 26 July, 1983.

The Times published her obituary. Representatives of those who had shared internment joined girls of the school at her funeral; 'Changi old girls' she called them. The cathedrals of Singapore and Kuala Lumpur, which have plaques in her memory, held services at which eloquent words were spoken in tribute to all that she achieved. Former pupils and others who had known her also joined in the praising of her life.

At the school there are now Foss Scholarships! Jalan Foss is still there. The time may come when the guide books will have to explain how the road got its name in a city that has almost eliminated all of the European names given to its streets.

The road leads to the site that she found for the Pudu English School – it now contains a secondary school with 2,100 pupils and two primary schools each with around 500 pupils, all flourishing. This is her living monument and the most enduring memorial. One imagines that she, too, would have thought so.

Some years later the BBC made a series about the internment of the women in Changi Prison. It was called *Tenko*. One of the characters was based on my Aunt Josephine; her character was called Joss (J Foss!) and the actress who played the part, Jean Anderson, bore a striking resemblance to her. They actually met while my aunt was being interviewed at the BBC, relaying her time of imprisonment – first-hand knowledge that was invaluable.

Sandy's: Nearly There!

After the slump of British pictures in 1922–23, my father's film career more or less came to an end. The British film industry was wavering due to the endless war and American dominance; it would rise again of course, but would take a little time. Dad, too, succumbed to TB yet again, and was now in hospital for some time. As he lay there in his hospital bed recuperating, he again wondered what his next move was to be.

He thought of many things – something would click no doubt. Suddenly, out of the blue, he was invited to produce a play in New York starring John Barrymore, the matinee idol of the time. Barrymore had been in England choosing a British actress to play opposite him. He eventually chose Fay Compton, a very popular actress of the time, and my father was to produce and direct it. Dad had been chosen especially for his noted work on the British stage and films. By good fortune he was now out of hospital and feeling his old self once again. This was 1922. It was quite an honour to be chosen by such a revered character as Barrymore, but of course my father was an expert at these things and had no qualms.

Rehearsals went well, so when he had an hour or two he wandered around New York to relax and reminisce about America. He had been there many times, but it was a fascinating city, so different from London. While wandering round the city, he noticed amongst other things small joints selling only sandwiches and coffee. Obviously started due to prohibition, they seemed very popular, and this intrigued him. And so the idea came to him: why not start something similar in London? Maybe on a slightly smarter scale – yes, this is what he would like to do. He knew so many famous people throughout his stage and screen career, they would all come to see what it was all about and no doubt help him get it started in any way they could.

The play ran its allotted time and was a hit, of course, because of the popularity of the Barrymores, the big names on Broadway at the time. John, his brother Lionel and sister Ethel were called the Royal Family of Broadway, so to speak, and later went on to become Hollywood stars, starring in films such as *Dr Kildare*. They could do no wrong. But Dad, with his first love firmly set on the stage professionally and proud to be part of the Barrymore package, was eager to try his hand at something new – something more personal. His mind was on a sandwich bar, as it was going to be. He was eager to get back to England and turn the dream into reality.

He was planning it all in his mind on his way back to Blighty on one of the many liners crossing the Atlantic. On arriving back to London, he was keen to get in touch with friends to tell them about his new dream and to look for a suitable venue. It had to be somewhere in the West End, of course! It had to be near all the theatres and showbiz happenings, in the heart of the action. Dad and his family were living in Chandos Street at the time, so nice and central!

But, as always happened, on his return to England he was yet again asked to produce numerous stage shows. So Sandy's, as the bar was to be named – after the Scots who he thought made the best sandwiches anywhere in the world – must wait a little longer. While he carried on working on his stage projects, he also continued looking for a suitable place to open Sandy's. It had to be right.

Eventually a plot in Oxendon Street, just off Coventry Street, became available: number twenty-five and right next door to the Prince of Wales Theatre, which was an ideal location with Piccadilly Circus just around the corner. The building had been an old army dumping ground during the War and would need a lot of work done to it, but everything was right and too good to turn down. The position was ideal and that was the main thing.

It wasn't long before the essential work got under way. He knew exactly how he wanted it to look, and it had to be artistic to the eye. My mother's brother, Tom, was an artist, so could help with that area. Then Dad was asked to produce a play, to write a sketch for a famous stand-up comedian and also to write a short play for the famous Japanese actor, Sessue Huyekedi, to perform at the Royal Command Performance at the Coliseum on 13 December, 1924.

The popular *The Stage* magazine said:

> On that day the King and Queen will be present to see numerous acts, including a syncopated Sonata band, dancers, the Griffith brothers, and Sessue Huyekedi on his first visit to London will appear with Denis Cowles and Ann Trevor in Kenelm Foss's dramatic playlet *The Knees of the Gods*.

The Stage later said:

> Sessue's acting was a revolution and powerfully realistic, and he created a profound impression on the audience.

After the applause, the introductions and the congratulations were given at the Command Performance. Dad was enthusiastic to get on with his new baby, Sandy's! Ideas were bouncing out of his head, so a new day was dawning. He knew instinctively in his bones it was going to be something big. It was, and it took London by storm.

Sandy's At Last

After the Royal Command Performance at the Coliseum in December 1924, my father rushed around to Oxendon Street the next morning to see how everything was going, and he was pleased to find things well in advance. Tom had designed the bar and the exterior to Dad's specifications; that was wonderful news. Not long to opening day, although there was still plenty to do, he had so many friends to help him, plus out-of-work actors and redundant soldiers all eager for a job after the War, and they would do any job, so there was no problem.

The London Pavilion, staging non-stop revues starring Noel Coward and all the big musical names of that time, was there too. This was the fabulous Roaring Twenties after all. What could be better?

Dad once remembered being in a bar with a friend and noticing how unappetising the sandwiches were there. 'God, I could do a lot better than that!'

'Well, why don't you then?' said a friend. 'Start up your own sandwich bar! That could be your next venture.' And here it was all happening! Glory be! Dad knew so many fillings for the sandwiches, remembered from Scotland and around the world. He had jotted them down, and more as they came into his head.

The start of Sandy's; press cuttings from 1925:

> Kenelm Foss in a new role! Sandwiches by magic! Famous actor opens a sandwich bar! Forsaking the stage for a shop! One of the most versatile men of the West End, actor, poet and playwright has opened a sandwich bar in theatre land. Those who know Kenelm Foss know that he does not hesitate when he has a good idea before carrying it into action!
>
> *Sunday Express*

'After nearly twenty-six years on the stage and film I find I can no longer make a living at my art. That is why I am now turning to trade and opening this sandwich shop in the very centre of the theatre world' – So said Kenelm Foss, the author, actor and producer in an interview today at his premises near to the Haymarket, where he opens a sandwich bar next Tuesday. The shop is an attractive little place designed by the producer himself, with mural drawings by many famous artists and cartoonists on the walls.

Over the fireplace is a painting by Cornforth and Gilson depicting the story of the origin of the sandwich: 'I realise,' said the producer of *Magic*, who has now effected a magical transformation of a more or less tumbledown shop, 'that people want food served quickly but not thrown at them. They also want it to be cheap and good. My object is to supply a public demand. I have to thank the many artist friends who have helped me attain my object in providing a rendezvous in the West End where people can have the best British food at reasonable prices and surroundings that are pleasing to the eye, which is the secret of gastronomic enjoyment.'

The *Star*

The bar was a very simple affair. It would be quite small, so as to have as much space as possible for the customers. The style of the actual eating area was a rounded bar for serving, continuing all the way to the door. Two small round tables attached to the floor in the centre, and then of course there were many high stools. The window area was to be simply and tastefully arranged with a jug of white Scottish heather in the centre. Outside was of course to be the 'Sandy Man' in full view, standing guard! (Later he was to be stolen but eventually returned.)

The kitchen in the cellar was furnished (once it had been cleaned) with a very large wooden table, a large stove and a very large sink – of course there were no fridges or dishwashers in those days. The Haymarket Stores (now defunct) were handily situated just across the road and were available for all the food needed – most importantly the bread. (Cut bread? In 1925 it was unheard of, but what an ingenious idea.)

Later, bread was delivered six times a day, so much was the demand! There was only Dad and my mother in the kitchen to start with and two friends in the bar, although very soon they had to find a 'washer upper'! Old Bill appeared on the first day as if by magic and stayed for ever. He seemed to love it and fitted in so well. He sang all the time but nobody seemed to mind. 'It's a Long Way to Tipperary' or 'If You Were the Only Girl in the World' were part of his repertoire. He actually had a rather good voice.

As it got busier, Ken realised that he had to have more help; so all those friends came in handy again, at least for the time being. He always had so many ideas for sandwich fillings. To start with there were twenty daily varieties, then eventually sixty, depending on the seasons. He was always in the markets first thing in the morning and across the road telling the manager of the Haymarket Stores all the exciting things needed for the day – and fast! Everyone got in the mood and it was a very happy time for all involved.

But back to the celebrity friends – how did they help? Well, they came in their hundreds. Knowing them, my father had cleverly invited them to the opening night by sending out gilt-edged invitation cards to each and every one of them. They came all right, but the bar was so small they couldn't all get inside! So, a huge queue formed outside, reaching right up to Coventry Street, unfortunately mingling with the queue for the Prince of Wales Theatre. The police had to be called to sort things out, but oh, the joy of it all! Wonderful and exciting days! But why 'Sandy's'?

'Well – Scotland makes the best sandwiches anywhere in the world,' said my father. 'And I should know, I ate them all the time when I was in Glasgow at the Repertory; they were wonderful. I have never forgotten them to this day! I found the Sandy Man in a junk shop while looking for something suitable to show outside, and anyway, I'm half Scottish, so there you are!' The Sandy Man soon became well-known and easy to see standing above the window outside.

Sandy's was a huge success from the word go, but obviously, apart from anything else, more room was needed. Dad had already decided to open a bar in Fleet Street by public demand, but No. 25 couldn't cope with the traffic of people! Dad knew No. 27 next door was empty. It, too, had been used as an army surplus store and shooting gallery, so a move there had to be arranged. The same people owned it who had sold No. 25 to him and they were quite amenable to let it go. So, 'with a little help from a friend', the new transaction was signed and sealed.

But to return to No. 25, Elizabeth said it was pure hell to start with in the kitchen. No one could have believed it would be so busy – they were not prepared. The demand was so great and each sandwich had to be made as ordered, never to be made in advance – that was the secret of the success, but difficult to handle if one hadn't enough hands to the pump!

Dad knew he would have to employ people as well as having his friends working for him. Within a couple of months he had eleven extra men working for him, which quickly made him realise that he now needed an office for all the paperwork that mounted up. The floor above the bar was luckily in fair order and was there to be used. After a quick lick of paint and a few desks and tables, things were soon in order!

My father also found a fellow to run the office – a really nice bloke who knew the ropes (so to speak). Percy Barbour was his name and he later became very useful to the whole family.

In one single week in 1926 it was calculated that 35,000 sandwiches were sold at the two branches (25 Oxendon Street and 65 Fleet Street). There were now 150 varieties to choose from and sixty daily (as in season) – 'Fast Food' was the new slogan! Fresh, appetising and nicely presented; one's order was ready almost before you could find a stool to sit on. Coffee was supplied by Fortnum and Mason. Jon designed the coffee mugs that had the name Sandy's stamped on to one side.

Right from the start, Sandy's was so busy and business was so good 'at the shop' that my parents had little time at home for cooking meals, especially on special occasions. I remember, that first Christmas, all of us (the family) strolling round to a French restaurant Dad knew in the Berwick market, just off Leicester Square. We were living in Chandos Street at the time, so it was not too far; we could see the Coliseum tower from the bedroom window. I cannot remember what we had to eat on that Christmas Day, but it all seemed rather jolly and exciting with the proprietor standing at the door to greet us! My father and Sandy's were big names in the news at the time, so we received the full treatment. I was only about seven or eight years old but can remember it all clearly.

Sandy's, 1925–1938

An amusing incident that happened one day at Sandy's: Two smart ladies strolled into the bar and one said to the other, 'What shall we have in our sandwiches today, Sweetie? Bath Chap? What is Bath Chap, Ken?'

'Pig's cheek, Madam.'

'Oh, I couldn't possibly eat pig's cheek. We'll just have ham!'

'Pig's bottom, Madam!' said Ken. With a smile.

While chatting to a reporter from the Glasgow *Sunday Mail* one day, my father said to him, 'Would you like to know the origin of the sandwich? It was invented by John Montague, the fourth Earl of Sandwich, who lived from 1718–1792. He was such an inveterate gambler that he was reluctant to leave the gambling table even for meals, so he asked a waiter to bring him some refreshment: a piece of meat between two pieces of bread. So this method of serving food was named after the inventor! If only he could see the varieties of sandwich fillings that one can get here in my bar now!'

Suffice to say that Sandy's tiny sandwich bars became a wow, growing all the time. Fleet Street had been the obvious second choice and was brimming over as soon as it opened. Patrons of Sandy's now even had a name for themselves – 'Sandyites' – and it was soon decided to open the Fleet Street branch twenty-four hours a day, as journalists needed sustenance any time of the day and night.

Soon after opening his numerous sandwich bars, Ken realised that a delivery service was required. People were enquiring whether Sandy's sandwiches could be delivered to offices and stores, as people could not always get out at lunchtime, or were too far away from the nearest bar. So, the famous Sandy Van was introduced (again lovingly designed by Ken and Tom) and soon became the focal point of interest and admiration whenever and

Family at Saltdean, about 1928. From left to right: Ken, Jon, Mick, Elizabeth, Fanny, Rosemary.

wherever it was seen. All deliveries were made within the hour of ordering, anywhere in London! This became a terrific success, as can be imagined.

The next thing to catch the imagination was the slogan, 'Where and What is Sandy's?' placed in every daily and evening newspaper and on the radio. It was an amazing and simple idea, but so effective. To artists at the London Pavilion revues, Sandy's proved very popular; they could just nip over the road to buy a sandwich – easy!

Noel Coward was appearing there at one time singing his popular song of the time, 'A Room With a View', and he too would pop over many times for a quick snack and to be seen! Prince Henry went to the revue one night, so it was said, and popped into Sandy's for a bite to eat – not bad publicity for Sandy's!

Later my father decided to have a cigarette machine installed, small and inconspicuous, near the door at No. 25, but there was often trouble! During one scuffle his wrist was broken, but cigarettes were very much 'the thing' in those days, so it was literally a must-have machine!

Once the Brighton branch was opened, Dad would arrange for us all to come and stay above the shop (there was a flat there). Percy Barbour would drive us all down, as Dad had bought a car but couldn't drive, so this is where Percy came in so handy to the family on these occasions. There was no sand at Brighton – although it was pleasant to sit on the beach there at times, which we did – but on the weekends we drove over to Saltdean, which is further along the coast and on the way to Rottingdean. There was lovely sand there – loads of it – and no beach to remark of, but broken bits of cliff here and there. I think we discovered Saltdean before Mr Butlin! The Palace Pier at Brighton was lovely then and fresh fish was sold on the beach every Sunday morning. I can hear the sellers now: ''Ere y'are lady. Lovely mackerel.' Good old Brighton, the lanes were so much better then as well. Happy memories indeed!

Here is another flattering article about my father and Sandy's from a London journalist:

A modern miracle of catering! He is a deuce of a chap, this Sandy fellow! Born just Kenelm Foss, he was not content with being a recognised power as an actor, novelist, poet, journalist, dramatist, scene designer and a producer of plays and films, but a few short years ago he must butt into the catering business as well and when Sandy Foss butts into anything, he butts in with some results!

Almost as soon as he opened his now famous sandwich bar beside the Prince of Wales theatre, it was a huge success. Starting off on a gross total of £50, famous friends of his – admiring his enterprise and grit – rallied around him any way they could. Sandy's soon became the meeting place for celebrated bohemians of all kinds. Apart from actors and artists, there were composers, musicians, journalists and novelists. Prominent folk of both sexes would come right out of their way to make a point of popping into Sandy's at any time of the day or night (up to midnight), sure of finding some kindred spirit present.

Rex Harrison said in his autobiography: 'We all went to Sandy's. It was the place to go and be seen in.'

I was only seven years old when the first Sandy's opened, but I remember it all vividly to this day. I was away at boarding school in Hertfordshire, Kings Langley Priory. A very trendy (way ahead of its time) school, being both co-educational and vegetarian, my brothers had been there too when they were younger. It was definitely the school to go to: a mixture of Heaven and Hell was what people called it! But I have happy memories of it.

There were many pets and farm animals (a donkey, ponies and goats) roaming around and large gardens and grounds that suited me, as I loved everything in that line. But when I was let loose during the holidays in Sandy's, that was the day! I had a ball, rushing around, upstairs past the loos on the mezzanine, poking my head in the office door.

I remember Barbour putting up with me; after all, I was the boss's daughter. Then downstairs I would go again, past the bar and into the kitchen for some yummy sandwiches, chatting with old Bill and singing with him. Oh, lovely days! Obviously this was a one-off and I didn't get to go there very often; soon afterwards we moved back to Hampstead yet again. But I loved it there too, and so did my mother, so pleased to be doing what she loved best: looking after the family. It was lovely to be near the heath again and Kite Hill.

My parents had had another daughter, Rosemary, in February 1924, being looked after by Mrs G, our grandmother, for a while (she was always there to help) while Elizabeth was busy in the kitchen in Sandy's. The family had moved house yet again, to a flat in Chandos Street just off the Strand, presumably to be nearer the shop – at least for the time being. In the early days, our mother had to walk home with the day's takings in her bag. I doubt if anyone would attempt that nowadays.

Jon was growing up now and was still at art school, but he was available to help in the bar whenever he could. He was an attractive asset, especially to the younger female customers. Mick was around and helped when he could in the office – very useful. He was always good at maths!

Of course, with success the office had to expand. With so many new branches to deal with, Ken had to employ a clerk, an office boy and a secretary. Julie was her name and she was rather attractive and good at her job. Also, Dad couldn't manage everything on his own indefinitely; he had to have associates and co-directors. Their names were soon under his on all the official documents. The kitchen now had trained staff for the unceasing demand of sandwiches. Coffee and orange juice were still the only drinks available, but there seemed to be no complaints!

In an article from the New York *Herald Tribune*, Elizabeth Craig, the famous food specialist and writer, wrote after she had tasted Sandy's wares:

> If leaving Piccadilly Circus in London Town and walking towards Leicester Square, you will come to Oxendon Street. On your right you will see Sandy's sandwich bars, painted in gold and faintly checked in blue and copper. This is the rendezvous for all those who know a good sandwich when they eat it. You cannot miss this favourite eating place for all the leading lights in the arts. There you will find, perched on high stools round the semicircular counter, or in little knots in the background, representatives of the stage, art, music, architecture, journalism and the films all waiting for their choice of sandwiches as eagerly as if they had ordered a banquet of costly viands replete with champagne.

She was by no means the only journalist to praise Sandy's:

> Sandy's had become so uncomfortably crowded that much larger quarters had to be acquired next door! And then too another bar had to be opened downstairs. This last one was to be a special portrait gallery, the decorations of which would consist of signed photographic portraits by Sasha and other distinguished artists on oak as before, all of highly distinguished 'Sandyites', as patrons of Sandy's love to call themselves. The result is, without exaggeration, unique in restaurant history.
>
> How has he done it, this Sandy man? Forty of Sandy's imitators have flopped in the West End alone in the last six years. What is Kenelm Foss's secret? Well, primarily it is originality. Ken was the definite initiator of the many varied sandwich bars in Great Britain. Starting with twenty different varieties a day, he now serves no less than sixty, including game as it comes into season. Originality, yes, and personality, and above all consistent value for money. The quality was and is good and has not deteriorated as so often happens with the march of success, and also pertinacity, for he is a deuce of a chap this Sandy fellow!
>
> Taken from Good Cheer, 1930

One day a young girl wandered into the original Sandy's; she looked very down. Dad noticed her sitting there on her own, so he strolled over with a coffee and asked her what the matter was.

'I feel so low,' she said. 'I want to become a writer, but do not know how to start. I can't even get any interviews. I just do not know what to do!'

They then chatted for a while and my father said he would see what he could do.

'I've got no money,' she said. 'Not even enough for this coffee.'

'It's my treat!' Dad said with a smile. 'But if you would like to earn a few pennies, how about clearing the plates and mugs and generally clearing up?'

The girl ended up staying most of the day and rather enjoyed it all. As well as her pocket money, she got a nice sandwich lunch. A few days later she came in again, smiling this time.

'I've got an interview and a job, and it's all thanks to you,' she said.

The girl and my father kept in touch and she would occasionally come in and Dad would hear all her news. Thus began the career of the well-known authoress, Marguerite Steen. She gave him a big write up in her autobiography, *Looking Glass*.

The opening of the bars at No. 27 was another huge occasion. The ground-floor bar was to be the same as next door, both of them having panelled walls, but the basement was to be completely different. It was named the 'Celeb' bar and was to be rather grander.

The oak panels were adorned with portraits of famous people who had posed for celebrated artists especially for Sandy's, and each one was signed underneath. This proved a great success; the public could go down and look at them, as long as they had bought a sandwich first! Bernard Shaw was one of the first to sign his name under his portrait. He had known my father for years and had relished many vegetarian delicacies invented for him. He left a note at the bar for Dad:

Dear Foss,

What is the use of an invisible signature? I have written my name in the left-hand corner, saying 'order vegetarian sandwiches' with my signature and date, but the inscription vanished as soon as the ink had dried. In certain lights the customers will be able to read it, if they lie on the floor on their backs and look sideways at it. On other occasions, they might just take your word for it.

Faithfully yours,

GBS

Edgar Wallace, looking rather like one of the gunmen in his thrillers, wrote: 'Portrait of me after Sandy had refused me my ninth farmer's relish.'

Farmer's relish by the way was a delicious sandwich served at Sandy's and a favourite of Shaw's too. It was just scrambled eggs mixed with mashed tomatoes – easy but very good! Another popular filling for one of Sandy's famous sandwiches was kedgeree: dried finnan haddock and newly laid hard-boiled eggs, with or without a mild curry sauce, and an optional salad. Duleepsinhji, the famous cricketer, liked them so much that he once ate fourteen at one sitting and then complained that he wasn't allowed any more!

> A special sandwich menu in celebration of the inauguration of Sandy's Celebrity bar at 27 Oxendon street, Haymarket on Monday June 9th 1928. Each celebrity is to obtain a special sandwich invented for him or her by Ken. There will also be some of the 'Sasha' portraits on the oak panels, each portrait especially signed and autographed by the said stars and will be the first time on view.

This invitation was sent out and the event was enthusiastically attended. Here are a few of the stars that came: George Bernard Shaw, the Countess of Oxford and Asquith, the Prime Minister Ramsay MacDonald, Sir Henry Wood, Edgar Wallace, John Galsworthy, Beverly Nichols, Noel Coward, Hannah Swaffer and Charlie Chaplin, who signed his portrait on the back of a £1 note, much to the amusement of everyone present.

Now that my father was 'in the money', so to speak, he was able to give his family a nice proper holiday. Not many folk went abroad in those days; only the ultra-rich went to the south of France. Even Noel Coward hadn't started the trend yet, but he did have a rather lovely house on the cliffs at St Margaret's Bay near Dover. Some of the well-known artists of the day also had houses there.

Gene Gerard would often be seen strolling along the sands and Jean Forbes Robertson had a house there too. She had recently made a big hit playing Peter Pan in the loveable J M Barrie play. So, of course the Fosses had to go there too! It was the place to spend your holidays and was rather lovely. The beach was good with plenty of sand at low tide. There was a small village at the top of the cliffs, St Margaret's at Cliff. To get there you had to climb up hundreds of steps, but one didn't seem to mind (quite an adventure really when you were young).

Of course, there was a long, winding road if you had a car! Percy Barbour drove us all down on these occasions to a lovely cottage – one of a row – right under the cliffs with sweet little gardens to sit in when not on the beach. Dad had leased the cottage for the whole month of August. It was heaven!

There was a large café there, selling, along with meals and snacks, all the usual bits and pieces. If you wanted anything else, it was up the steps to the village! But there were shrimps – masses of them on the sands at low tide – and the sea went out for ever. One could walk to Dover and back and the tide would still be out. Sometimes we did just that. You could hire nets to drop in the pools as you walked round the white cliffs. Then a look in the shops, a bite for lunch and, on returning, pick up the nets that were now brimming with shrimps. Shrimps for tea! Delicious!

The sea at St Margaret's was notorious for jellyfish, so there were many rafts dotted around for swimmers to make for when the stingers were after them. I can remember my sister and I along with our dog of the time, Fossie, sitting on a raft watching the hoards of jellyfish milling around. How we got back to the beach I don't know, but I never remember being stung. St Margaret's Bay was (and is) the nearest point to France in Britain, so it was used, for obvious reasons, during World War Two. For anyone who knew it before then (as I did), it is not quite the lovely place now as one remembers it, sadly. As they say, never go back!

Meanwhile, Sandy's was still flourishing, more bars cropping up all over London: one in Charing Cross opposite the Whitehall Theatre and others in strategic places such as Mark Lane and No. 1 Castle Court, Birchin Lane – quite apart from the one in Fleet Street which had opened a few years earlier. The Sandy's bar in Bouverie Street was open day and night for journalists who needed sustenance at all times, and of course, there was one in Brighton. There was also talk of Sandy's in Manchester and Glasgow (they would have liked that!) and even Paris; wonderful and exciting talk but...

Even our friends in New York were interested and the odd American visitor would sometimes pop into Sandy's while in London. My father once said to a reporter:

> While once entering my little sandwich shop, I noticed two Americans who were reading the sign outside, which with modesty spoke of twenty varieties daily, and pausing on the steps one said to the other:
> 'Yes, but I'll bet you a greenback to a nickel they haven't got the only sandwich that tastes good outside a desert!'

I was interested, therefore, when this thoroughly American gentleman in search of a light lunch asked, 'Have you got an American club sandwich, Mister?'

'In five minutes, Sir!' I said with a smile.

There was complete astonishment on the American's face as he turned to his friend and said, 'Five minutes, boy, and I was thinking we would have to row home to get one!' And with one of those twists of a very expressive American epigram, he said, 'Well, Mister, I'm in a hurry for it until I get it, then she can go slow!'

Now, an American club sandwich has in it half the breast of a chicken, bacon, tomato, lettuce and three pieces of thin toast. It is served as hot as can be and coffee with it is a delight! So you had the producer who first produced Chesterton's play *Magic* in other surroundings, producing this tasty product of his sandwich hobby! Snacks at these bars, by the way, were now considered smarter than eggs and bacon or kippers after the theatre, and all smart folk congregated there between eleven and twelve each night!

You wouldn't think my father, as well as running his sandwich bars, would have time to write books, but he did. His latest novel, *Nuncs' Causeway*, was a bohemian fantasy by the greatest bohemian of them all.

> He knows bohemia as only those can who are in it or of it.
>
> Critic's report

> Disagreeing with Mr Chesterton's dog 'Quoodle' who said of the human being that 'they ain't got no noses', Mr Foss has invented a club for noses, or in bohemian terms, 'Nuncs'. Each with their individual noses are eight members of the Nuncs Club, for which the qualifications are poverty and failure, two ingredients that don't always make for unhappiness in bohemia! That Mr Foss knows well! His description of young life's willing sacrifice to home is charmingly told and the loyal Nuncs sticking together through thick and thin, championing each other's causes, applauding each other's failures, gives a true and vivid impression of the real camaraderie existing among the bohemians of all time.
>
> Description of the book by the publishers, Humphrey Toulmin

The causeway that gives the title of Mr Foss's new novel its name is the way between Adelphi Terrace and the Green Room Club in Leicester Square. Mr Foss has many fantastical, whimsical and delightful things to tell us about Bohemian London.

Daily Mirror

The author of *Nuncs' Causeway* is a man of amazing versatility. An old Malvern boy, he studied art in Paris and exhibited his watercolours and sketches on many occasions, which were highly praised. To most people he is best known for his sandwich bars in the West End of London, but not to be outdone, apart from writing novels and being in command of Sandy's, he has found time to return to the stage, playing Charles the Second in Cosmo Hamilton's *Gentlemen, the King*.

Passing Show, 1929

But it was not his intention to return permanently to the stage: 'My sandwich bars have enabled me to devote time to do other things I really want to do.'

Whether Foss likes selling books, acting on the stage or selling sandwiches best, that is the question – some of each, it seems!

Sporting Times

Kenelm Foss's new novel *Nuncs' Causeway* is having great success with the reading public! Especially in Scotland, which has fond memories of him when he was at the Royal Repertory Theatre in Glasgow.

Glasgow News, 1929

Soon after the end of the Cockran Revues in the West End (Edward the Prince of Wales was a big fan of the Revues Noel Coward was in, and was often seen there. He especially enjoyed and admired Noel's two hit songs, 'A Room with a View' and

'Mad about the Boy'), while enjoying his usual sandwich in Sandy's, Noel told my father he was going to tour Malaysia with a group of young artists (Johnny Mills included, he was a song and dance man in those days).

While out there, Noel thought up an idea for a play for himself and Gertie (Lawrence). He wired her at the time, but she wasn't too thrilled with the idea. When he returned and they had discussed it, however, she changed her mind. They started rehearsing straight away and a theatre was found nearby. The name of the play? *Private Lives*! The rest, as they say, is history.

Who could ever forget that wonderful balcony scene, the two of them standing there either side of a small partition between apartments. A very young and almost unknown Laurence Olivier played her second husband. A small quote from the now famous words: Elyot (Noel): 'You don't hold any mystery for me darling, do you mind? There isn't a particle of you I don't know, remember and want! I want you back again, Amanda.' She replies: 'Don't, don't, you're making me cry so dreadfully!' And then there follows the lovely song 'Someday I'll Find You' – brilliant! We, the family, had a record of that scene and I can remember it word for word to this day. The other side of the record was Noel and Gertie singing 'Someday I'll Find You' as a duet.

Meanwhile, suddenly Julie was on the scene. Yes, Julie from the office at No. 25, and our life changed! Well, a little. Dad hadn't been around much by then (with the family, I mean). He had either been filming all hours of the day and night, getting ill or going abroad for months on end, and that was before Sandy's! After that, things didn't ease up as running the bars took for ever. Anyway, when Sandy's had started out, Mother had been very useful in the kitchen, making endless sandwiches, but eventually, when Ken had acquired trained staff, she was happy to be just a mother. We were moving again from Hampstead via Kings Langley in Hertfordshire to Watford, nearer my sister's and my schools; that was the reason this time, I believe!

I met Julie once or twice in the office at No. 25 whenever I went there, and once even stayed with her and my father in their charming little cottage at Waltham St Lawrence in Berkshire. In the naïve way of an eleven year old, it seemed perfectly natural.

Then suddenly Dad wanted a divorce! Our poor mother just wished things could stay as they were; they had been apart for quite some time by then, things didn't matter to her any more, but she hated the idea of being dragged through the courts. I suppose it all went through, but there again it all seemed to pass over our heads.

Things, they were a'changing everywhere. It was now the thirties, quite a different kettle of fish – rumblings in Europe. But the film business in Britain had revitalised itself. Numerous talented actors and directors were arriving from the continent for obvious reasons; people who had been known in their own countries. Alexander Korda for one, soon to make a big impact over here (later he married Merle Oberon) with many famous films and well-known actors and actresses; also Paul Zinner and his wife Elizabeth Bergner, who made the popular film, *Escape Me Never* together. The name of the main character in the film was Gemma, soon to become a very popular name for girls over here. Then of course there were Herbert Wilcox and Anna Neagle making popular films, so it wasn't all bad!

There were 'talkies' of course now, and colour, so things were looking up! Not that my father seemed interested any more. Been there, done that, to coin a phrase! But the unique atmosphere of the twenties had gone, slipped away without people realising it, taking with it the exciting and colourful lively feeling that had engulfed everyone then. It was sad, but nothing could be done about it.

But times kept changing, and they would never be the same again – not for a long time anyway. Sandy's was still there and seemed as popular as ever, but there were cracks appearing. Trouble was brewing at the Brighton branch; it was crying out for help but no one noticed it in time. It seemed that Ken didn't want to know – he probably couldn't believe it – until it was too late. The truth was that those in charge, to put it crudely, were fleecing him. He was always in London and had so many branches to manage that Brighton got put aside.

Now Ken had to rush down there in double-quick time to try to sort things out. It took weeks to probe out the truth and sadly by then there was nothing that could be done. Dad couldn't chance it any more; closing the bar was the only option. It was horrendous – and sad for all of us too, especially now that we were older, for we loved popping down to dear old Ship Street, Brighton! Not to have a Sandy's there seemed unbelievable!

Our father had to now be on his guard, which was a worry. He wanted everything to run smoothly, and people to be trustworthy and honest (some hope). No more talk of other branches opening, it seemed he had to keep an eye on what he'd got! Anyway, it appeared he was into the theatre again (a little bit anyway) if he was wanted, and he was definitely wanted!

He was approached to produce numerous plays. The first chosen was *Paganini*, written by David Wells, the pen name of an old friend of his who was also playing the lead role: Ernest Milton. It was being presented at the Whitehall Theatre on matinees only, for a short tryout. Ernest had written it with a clear idea of where his own powers lay. The scene was laid in Paris 1837–40 and is the story of the great violinist, Paganini.

The next production was to be *Sonata* written by a new playwright, Evelyn Millard, and was to be presented twice nightly at the Cambridge Theatre, having already been on tour. My father was kept busy producing numerous matinee plays (the new trend), not forgetting Sandy's, which needed an eye kept on it – no easy task!

These names make news! A comeback!

William Hickey

Once well-known as a dramatist and producer and writer for British films in their early days, Kenelm Foss has returned to the stage temporarily. He is producing *Paganini* next Friday at the Whitehall theatre. A highly emotional producer, his limbs tremble at the crises in the drama, tears stream readily from his eyes. It was he who brought Chekhov's *Cherry Orchard* to London. When he left the theatre and films he founded the famous chain of sandwich bars, Sandy's; sixty varieties daily. 'Chief trouble,' he says, 'you can't copyright sandwiches! Rivals imitate them. The Scots, now they were the best sandwich makers in the world!'

Daily Express, 23 January, 1935

> I have often heard it said that the stage is one of the hardest professions to give up. Mr Foss is a case in point! Some years ago he left the theatre and films to establish in the West End the first and best of sandwich bars. Now I hear he is coming back to the stage as a producer; that is the job in which he always excelled. He got his hand in by producing the newest special matinees of *Paganini* and I am delighted to hear this is only a beginning. The play with which one always associates Foss is Chesterton's *Magic*, which I should say is fully due for a revival.
>
> 'Talk of the Town', *Evening News*, 2 February, 1935

Dad just couldn't keep away when offered a part! But while the cat's away the mice will play. Bad managers, unscrupulous people and jealous employees were letting him down. It was all suddenly happening, and too quickly! It wasn't Nos. 25 and 27; they were the main assets. They were keeping everything going! It was unbelievable to even contemplate that this fantastic, fabulous idea of his was slipping through his fingers without him knowing. This haven of the famous was disappearing before his eyes. This wonderful place that he had invented and nurtured, surely it wasn't about to fold.

Dad just wanted things to carry on without problems (some hope of that). That sort of thing just doesn't happen, not often or for long anyway – especially if you take your eyes off it for a second. All the time his rivals (enemies) were stealing all his sandwich ideas, although he had discovered this was happening some time before.

The opposition opened bars blatantly similar to Sandy's. Had they no shame? No, of course not, and thankfully most of them failed. But did they think it easy? More fools them. However, none of this helped. Unfortunately, there's no copyright on sandwiches.

Suddenly things began to change. War was looming, and these were dreadful worrying times. With so many horrors happening in Europe, we knew it was just a matter of time for us in isolated Britain. It was a worrying time, too, in the theatre, as one can imagine – very unsettling. Sandy's was still going strong, or so everyone thought at the time. It had opened in 1925 and now here it was, eleven or twelve years later, still as popular as ever – or so it seemed.

Dad was such a clever fellow, so good at a lot of things. Everything he touched turned to gold, whatever he did. After a shaky start; when money was scarce in the early theatre days; when he wondered if anything would ever materialise for him. Then things suddenly got underway and he could do no wrong, getting to the top with ease. But, dare I say it, he became sick of things.

'Well, I've done what I wanted to do, now what's next?'

He thought like this – especially when everything was running smoothly and without problems – but suddenly here he was with problems at Sandy's without even realising it. He didn't want anything to go wrong or for there to be any hassle; he couldn't handle anything like that, but things were wrong with knobs on!

He had been the big star of the film world while he was there, and could do no wrong. They'd never had anyone like him before, a lot to do of course with his many years of stage training. But being ill for long periods didn't help; people forget and manage without one! Thus with Sandy's, after a time, when things were running smoothly, he thought: 'Well, nothing much to do here at the moment, so I'll do a play!'

While he was away, things were going from bad to worse at Sandy's. Half the branches were losing money by fair means or foul, with just the Oxendon and Fleet Street branches keeping things going. If only he had stuck to the original three, maybe none of this would have happened. How many times have people said such things? It all seemed such a good idea at the time, and where has one heard that before? A board meeting was called and all Ken's co-directors demanded a vote; it was six to one. The books just weren't adding up; there was not enough money coming in and now no money in the kitty. So it was decided before things got worse that the whole conglomeration should be sold. Dad was a broken man. His dreams had come to an end.

Soon after the demise of Sandy's, my mother, brother Jon and I were in London to see a play, *Sweet and Low*. The 'in' play of the time, it was a subtle light comedy starring Hermione Gingold. We walked down Oxendon Street out of curiosity, glancing into Sandy's as we passed. It was lunchtime and around midday, but the bar was completely empty; all the glamour and atmosphere had gone. We felt rather pleased it was empty, guiltily, but sad as well while we remembered the good old times. 'You've either got it or you haven't!' Mum said.

The only things that kept Dad sane were his books. He was just meeting the deadlines on his latest biography, *Here Lays Richard Brinsley Sheridan*. It was published in early 1939, sold well and had good notices, as all his books did. Now that he had more time on his hands, he could spend some of it at the British Museum, swotting up on all the subjects he was to write about. He also wrote sketches for stand-up comedians, for the music halls and for radio. These acts were very popular at the time; people were desperate for some light comedy in those dreary days as war quickly approached. But what next? He'd think of something, and he did...

Chish and Fipps (1938–39)
Ensa and Out (1939–45)

After the shock of Sandy's, Dad did the odd play, not being one to sit about moaning for long, but nothing spectacular. He had been living in a fairly remote, but very attractive, village in Berkshire – Waltham St Lawrence – but after his break-up from Julie, his lady friend, he moved to Maidenhead just down the road, and once more began to wonder what to do with the rest of his life! The village around that area only had little local shops for provisions. There was hardly any transport available in that area, with very few cars around in those days. So how about a mobile fish and chip delivery van?

What a brilliant idea! Yet again he had thought of something no one else had. So, again, he gathered his friends and associates around to tell them all about it and ask for their thoughts. Unsurprisingly, they were all for it. So organisations started again and it did not take too long. Of course, permission had to be granted and many people thought he was mad! They would, because they had not thought of it themselves. No, his ideas were never mad!

After organising, negotiating, fussing and worrying for months to get every detail spot on, things were starting to get settled. Dad had even handily found a little disused building at the side of the railway station for fish and potato deliveries. The building was also to be used to peel and slice potatoes; it even had a small annex for a little office. Hot fish and chips delivered to your door (except for very special occasions), near enough. The van was decorated and painted of course, and would park on the corner nearest the main houses and cottages in the village. Just what the people wanted on a cold Friday night, or any other day for that matter. Fish and chips beautifully cooked and piping hot.

The firm was to be called Chish and Fipps – what a great

name. Of course, capable men had to be found and trained, which was always hard but never impossible; the men not only had to drive but to cook as well. In fact, there were many people offering their services, surprisingly. So, before long, things were under way. He had two vans to start with, just to see how things went, and the public repaid the faith by warmly welcoming the idea. They were fantastically pleased, and praised and thanked Dad and his assistants for thinking up such a brilliant idea and getting it on its way. It seemed like a dream come true, and for almost a year everything went well.

Praise was heaped on the venture from all over the country, with other villages asking, 'Why not us? We want fish and chips delivered to us. Why has such a brilliant idea not been thought of before?' What could ever go wrong? Well, one of the vans catching on fire and going up in smoke for a start! (I remember reading about it in the newspapers.) The driver was badly burned, but not fatally, luckily. This was not a good omen. There was big insurance to be dealt with, obviously, and the police were involved with warnings and questions.

The public did not want to lose this wonderful thing that had happened to them, of course; they had got used to the idea of hot meals being delivered to their doors! My father and their friends had naturally assumed they had thought of everything – amazingly, a problem like this had never been visualised. It became obvious that vans catching fire in out-of-the-way places with help nowhere near put paid to another of his bright ideas. It was a great loss as well, money-wise, so it was back to the drawing board – I think not. Dad had got sick of thinking up new ideas and them going wrong, especially if they went as badly wrong as Chish and Fipps.

It was about this time that Fidelle came on the scene; Fido to all the family. She was tall, dark, very attractive and full of fun, and we all got on very well together. By this time Dad had moved back to his beloved Hampstead. Luckily for us, it was much easier to get to. Fido was well into astrology, so about ten years later, when my son Brian was born, she got in touch with me straight away asking me about the time of the birth, date, hour, right down to the minute and second. She explained that she had exciting vibes about the birth, so, on being told, she predicted that he would do well in his life and go far, which happily has all come true. Fido could drive and had a car, so that was a nice bonus for them. Dad had never learnt or shown any interest in driving for himself.

It was around that time, as so often happens in life, that fate stepped in. World War Two was looming and things changed dramatically. The war eventually started on 3 September, 1939. ENSA (Entertainment National Service Association), seeing it all coming, was well-prepared and beckoned! So that added another string to Dad's bow. He joined straight away, on the administration side mainly, but sometimes presented and even acted in small shows in campsites around the country, while many others of course – including actors, singers and directors – travelled all over the world entertaining the troops.

Life was pretty settled and enjoyable for the next four or five years. During the War, Jon (my brother) was in the Air Ministry. He had been at the Slade School of Art, so he was well-equipped to design posters, with slogans such as 'Join the RAF' and 'Join the WRAF'. Dad was very proud of this, as we all were. I can remember seeing the posters on the walls of post offices around the country and boasting about them to all and sundry.

The big attraction at the time was Vera Lynn, who quickly became the forces' sweetheart with her wonderful strong singing voice and rendition of many popular songs. Who could ever forget her singing 'White Cliffs of Dover' and We'll Meet Again'? Troops all over the world could not get enough of her, calling for more wherever she went. Dad always kicked himself for not rushing to become her manager!

After the War, Dad decided to take things easy. After all, he had had an amazing career spanning over thirty years. His life had been full and varied, but he still continued to write books, mostly biographies of famous people: Sheridan, Beardsley and Turner, amongst others. This kept him nicely busy, and the British Museum became almost a second home for a few years! He had a calm and pleasant retirement, which, after his amazing life, was all he could have asked for.

Kenelm Foss, 1885–1963

On 28 November, 1963, the death of my father was announced on the radio. Lewis Casson, the actor and long-time friend of his, spoke many kind words about Dad that morning, words which were highly appreciated by all of our family.

Memories of my father personally, family-wise; what can I say? As far as I remember, we were always happy. He was a fun man, always jolly and laughing. We had nice holidays – nothing too grand, but always memorable. He was always so busy when we were young, but was always there for us at the right times: Christmas, holidays and on special occasions.

No regrets.

Quotes – July 1926

King Edward VII's favourite sandwich is also the pet recipe of Kenelm Foss the actor, film and play director, now incidentally the proprietor of Sandy's Sandwich Bar, a West End resort patronised by Bohemian London. 'Although I am an enthusiastic fan of all sandwiches, from the conventional or railway ham to the most American devised meat between two pieces of toast, my own special favourite is a certain cheese sandwich which was also the favourite of the late King Edward. His chef put me on to it and told me that woe betide him if a supply was not available during shooting parties or a visit to the races. The filling, which is best between brown bread without butter, consists of fifty per cent grated stilton cheese – it must be ripe, but dry – and thirty-five per cent finely chopped celery, plus a hint of parsley,' said Kenelm.

'Could you make me, say, half a dozen different kinds of sandwiches?' asked the Tit Bits man as he sat at the counter of Sandy's – Kenelm Foss, who has opened this Sandwich Bar in the West End of London, knows of ninety-six different kinds! Mr Foss, who serves sandwiches when he is not cutting them, told him his entry into the catering business was partly due to a wager! 'I told a friend (whilst we sat in a dingy bar) I'd like to show them how to run a Sandwich Bar – I also saw places in New York that gave me ideas, but the supreme sandwich makers are the Scots – I have tasted sandwiches at a shop in Glasgow that could not be equalled anywhere else in the world.' Amongst his ninety-six varieties are sandwiches with fillings of sheep's tongues, boars' heads, hare, wild duck, pig's cheek, quail and grouse, when in season – but the most popular on the menu is kedgeree: dried finnan haddock and new hardboiled eggs plus a salad if required. Another favourite is hot roast beef. Almost any drink goes with a sandwich, but the most agreeable is undoubtedly coffee. Customers will have fresh sandwiches and the only way for this is to make them as required; the bakery man calls six times a day.

Sandy, whose real name is Kenelm Foss, the famous actor, author, poet and producer of plays and films and who is of

Scottish and Welsh descent has also immortalised the ubiquitous British sandwich (Beef) in a glass case in an alcove to the side of the counter, where patrons who sample his wares can see from what he has saved them! A 'No tinned food, no foreign produce' sign is prominently displayed and another sign facing you when you order says, 'When there is a crush will you Sandyites please pay for your grub as you get it.' All orders are ready in a few minutes.

Sandy's has now become the 'in place' for celebrities to linger, especially to catch up on all the famous etchings and drawings on the walls. 'My friends from the Savage Club were my first patrons, then my friends from Fleet Street discovered what I'd done and trekked along, then the artists and my stage cronies and now not only is this nothing more or less than an up-to-date Sandwich Bar, but a sort of club for friends to meet over a snack and a cup of coffee as well,' says Mr Foss.

Notes on My Father's Film Career

My father, who was now running the fabulously successful Sandy's sandwich bars in London, was approached by the *Sunday Mail* to write his film memoirs of the various personalities he had known connected with the British film industry (1914–1924):

> Not only was Kenelm an actor and author, but one of the best-known film producers in the industry. Formally associated with the Glasgow Repertory Theatre, he has pioneered in British pictures for many years. The fun, the thrills and intimate studio associations with many famous stars are set down for the first time in the newspaper. Dealing with the circumstances in which he began, he tells how he met many noted producers in the early days, including the genius Maurice Elvey and later D W Griffiths, the noted American whom he met on one of his numerous trips to New York. He also worked with many noted actors and technicians of that time period, including Maurice Moscovitch and Victor McLaglen and others too numerous to mention. Most of these stars have passed through his hands at one time or another and there is probably no character in the business with which he had not rubbed shoulders, and obtained entertaining recollections of – meekly obeying the raucous commands of his megaphone.

To return to Maurice Elvey, the brilliant film producer who brought so much to British films, he had an alert intelligence and radiated a remarkable personality. It was through him that Ken actually entered films, meeting him one day in London, and taking up his suggestion to meet him the next day in the studios. The rest as they say—

My father had been at that time at a loss to know exactly what to do with the rest of his life (he was actually only twenty-eight years of age at the time) after a number of years producing plays at the Glasgow rep. and running the Little Theatre in London along which lowbrows called highbrow lines. G K Chesterton had written the play *Magic* especially for him and he had made a hit of it, produced a never-before-seen play of Bernard Shaw's and presented the first performance of *Damaged Goods* in England. In a word, when World War One broke out, with his record in Glasgow and the Little Theatre he was branded as an intellectual producer, and the public knew that intellectual producers were not in demand in the early days of the War. What they wanted was light entertainment i.e. *A Little Bit of Fluff* and subsequently *Chu Chin Chow*. Amazingly enough, soon after he had taken the plunge into films at Elvey's suggestion, the first thing he was invited to produce was *A Little Bit of Fluff*, but no matter. Well nobody had wanted him at that time, not even Lord Kitchener, for he was in very poor health and had originally left Glasgow with TB, so meeting Elvey was a godsend, and he took his offer with open arms.

When he first entered films, the poor British picture industry was holding up its head quite well, thank you, against the United States. The two nations were at that time competing on more or less equal terms. In 1914, however, the little accident of a war occurred to us, but not to our American film rivals until 1917, which gave them three good years in which to corner the world market. They did so effectively and they will never be ousted until the powers that be look after the British film industry as jealously as Uncle Sam suckles his, greatly to the advantage of his National Exchanger. No, it's the money that does it every time – money for new studios, for research, for training of stars and for buying over the heads of alien competitors' best-selling books rights of British authors, etc. However, the British are now pulling themselves up again, as we always do.

In New York once, when Dad was trying to market some of the pictures he had made in England, he certainly only met film folk. True, but oh dear he heard enough adverse criticism of himself, our unfortunate country, our pictures and our insignificant contribution to the War to last him a lifetime. But not, I might add, from D W Griffiths. Dad was lucky enough while on a visit to New York to be able to watch him directing a film on Marnaronde Island. He had heard him described as a showman swanker and lacking in any sense of humour. He could only say that he found him most courteous and modest and kind enough to express what appeared to be quite a genuine interest in my father's own poor productions and possessions with a considerate and quiet sense of humour. They met only in the studios and he struck Dad as being almost shabby in the picturesque bohemian fashion. And Dad was glad to see that both his studio management and directors were British, as well as several of his actors, despite the misconception that the British compatriots were supposed to be such duds with everything connected with the silver screen.

Dad had written the book *Till Our Ship Comes In* some time before he entered films, so was very pleased when it was chosen as the subject for a six-reel weekly film show, the first of its kind. The book was actually published at the same time, so got quite a lot of publicity. He not only wrote it, he was playing the lead and producing it as well – a truly one-man show. It was being presented by the Q film studios and is indeed a unique production. And Q films must be congratulated for an excellent show.

> It's the story of a doctor and his family who always lived in hope that the future would smile on them one day.
> One of the most versatile men in film today, Kenelm Foss has written scenarios for almost every British studio. He produced his own picture plays, adapted and directed scores of popular works in a variety of pictures familiar to the public, and he is now engaged in a steady fight for all British films.
>
> *Daily Mail*, 17 November, 1919

More memories. The ever-enthusiastic Alfred Wareing – who ran the Glasgow Repertory Theatre (now sadly defunct) – and Dad were friends for many years, and it was he who put Dad on his feet from the very start. When Dad was only just out of his teens and a long way from home, Graham Moffet and his wife were at the Glasgow Rep at the same time as he was, before going on to greater things – as were so many big stars-to-be, who all enjoyed their stay there. One person in particular Dad remembered was Cyril Maude. He had directed him in his stage success in London, in the play *The Headmaster*. He was now to direct him in the film version; how excellent he was in that part and what a charming man he was to work with. It was indeed due to his delightfully friendly personality that the film company engaged him for the picture of that play. It became such a completely happy family that he was able to complete the film in double-quick time. It was done sooner than those in control dreamed and Maude did not want to accept his full fee. It was only when Dad pointed out that finishing the film early had saved hundreds of pounds in staff, overheads and retakes that he consented to take it.

Ken worked happily with so many stars: Percy Marment, Milton Rosma, Jean Cadell, Dorothy Minto, and many more. Apart from a few minor exceptions, he could honestly say his film career was a very happy one. Then again, he mustn't forget to thank Maurice Elvey for letting him put his foot in the door in the first place.

Newspaper Quotes: October 1928
Acting Again – Couldn't Keep Away

It is heard that the new Duchess Theatre off Drury Lane is to open, with its first play to be *Gentlemen, the King*, a romantic comedy about the days of Charles II and mainly about the twenty-four hours preceding his return to England in 1660. The entire action takes place in Flanders. Percy Marment (the well-known film star) as the penniless fugitive monarch, while another outstanding character in the play is Dick Pym, an impudent swashbuckling actor who goes around impersonating His Majesty. This was not an easy part to cast, but the choice fell ultimately to Kenelm Foss, whose Pistol in *Henry V*, and Cyrano had made on Marment a lasting impression.

Kenelm Foss is coming into the limelight again. He is now playing in Cosmo Hamilton's play *Gentlemen, the King*, and I hear that Cayme Press is about to publish his new novel *Nuncs' Causeway*, which is described as a bohemian fantasy and deals intermittently with theatrical life. I have not seen Foss for some time; the last time I think was in Sandy's sandwich bar, just behind the Prince of Wales Theatre. He started these sandwich bars a couple of years ago; they are so popular in the West End that he is able to return to his first love, the stage. He started with Granville Barker in the famous Court theatre season, and for some years was the chief producer in the Glasgow Repertory Theatre. His greatest achievement was the presentation of Chesterton's delightful play *Magic*, which he produced under his own management at the Little Theatre. His novel should give some interesting and authentic glimpses of the theatre.

The Stage, 1928

A character with Shakespearean qualities is Pym, the boisterous impersonator of the king played by Kenelm Foss in the new play *Gentlemen, the King* at the Duchess theatre. His fine sense of low comedy earned him immense applause. Mr Foss, a Shakespearean actor of repute, has a part which calls for adroit handling and his experience should stand him in good stead.

Daily Express, 1928

Mr Foss gave a very satisfactory interpretation of the swaggering Pym, it was a difficult role and that it was made convincing says much for the acting of Mr Foss.

Daily Express

Kenelm Foss continues to stick to the stage while the sandwich empire runs itself. His play *Second Fiddle* is to be presented at the Q theatre on a Monday in February 1927.

Evening Standard

Second Fiddle is a play, as the title suggests, about music. It contains picturesque characters. Here is a composer of serious music who is ordered to make a living in writing jazz tunes as the ghost of an utterly unusual but very business-like person. Here is his contact with the real world; an admired cast makes a very pleasant evening.

Sunday Express, 1927

Kenelm Foss's novel *Nuncs' Causeway*, just out, is about London's Bohemia, by one who knows it! As an old member of the Savage Club he has in turn been an art student in Paris, actor, stage producer, poet, journalist, screen designer, press agent, dramatist, and caricaturist, and as such is probably better-qualified than most to write about Bohemian London today. The Causeway that gives the title to Mr Foss's novel is the way between Adelphi Terrace and the Green Room club in Leicester Square. Mr Foss has intimate knowledge of the actors of Nuncs' Causeway and so represents much first-hand observation of a lively picture of Bohemian life in London today. As presented, all the characters are imaginary with few exceptions, which are specified.

Passing Show, 1929

Kenelm Foss, the author of *Nuncs' Causeway*, is a man of amazing versatility. An old Malvern boy, he studied art in Paris and exhibited on many occasions, and then he has been actor, film star, stage producer of highbrow drama and has also published novels and volumes of verses, but to a large section of the public he is best known on account of his sandwich bars and the Celebrity bar in Oxendon Street. Mr Foss is at present playing Pym in *Gentlemen, the King* at the Duchess Theatre.

Passing Show, 1928

Fanny Burney

Fanny Burney, the famous authoress (I am her namesake and proud of it), 1752–1840, was best known as the author of *Evelina* which was one of the most engaging novels of the eighteenth century. For much of her long life she was an incomparable diarist, the first royal reporter, witnessing both the madness of George III and the birth of Queen Victoria. She lived most of her life in Surrey, England: a childhood in Chessington, in the house of Samuel Crisp, which became her favourite home, then after her marriage to a French nobleman, M D'abley (who lost his family seat in the French Revolution) they lived first in Michelham, then at Humble, a small hamlet between Dorking and Leatherhead, where on the house, to this day, can be found a plaque stating 'Fanny Burney lived here'. They afterwards moved to Bookham, where she bore her husband a son, at the late age of forty-two, on whom she doted. She was a protégée of Dr Samuel Johnson, who praised her novel to the skies. She was so pleased when she heard this that she danced a little jig around the room in front of all the dignitaries present, much to their amusement. The famous playwright, Richard Brinsley Sheridan, was one of her greatest friends.

Works of Kenelm Foss

Plays Produced and Directed

1903   *Jack A Dreams*

1904   *Hippolytus / Where There Is Nothing / John Bull's Other Island* (played lead)

1905   *Merry Wives of Windsor / Dandy Dick / One More Day / The Money Spinner / Shades of Night / Trichinae / One Summer's Day / The Wild Duck / Votes for Women / The Return of the Prodigal / A Country Mouse / The Man of Destiny*

1906   *Harlequin King / Brigadier Gerard / Othello / Lady Inger of Ostrat / The Bondman* (Drury Lane)

1907   *The Bondman* (Adelphi) */ The Prodigal Son / Salome / Prunella*

1908   *The Marriages of Mayfair* (Drury Lane)

1909   *Merry Wives of Windsor / Le Malade Imaginaire / Mrs Gorringe's Necklace / Croydon Fantastics / Tried and True / Twelfth Night / Two Gentlemen of Verona / John Bull's Other Island / The Marriages of Mayfair* (tour)

1910   *The Truth About Dr Courtney* (Glasgow) */ The Last Man / Augustus in Search of a Father / Admiral Guinea* and *Barbara Grows Up / What the Public Wants* (Carlisle) */ Nan / The Twelve Pound Look / Justice / Dandy Dick / Jean / Prunella / The Great Duke of Florence / Colin in Fairy Land / Pride of Life*

1911   *The Little Stone House / The Passing of Talmer / Nan* (revived) */ The Three Wayfarers / Interior / Pantaloon / The Marriage of Columbine / The Cutting of the Knot / Carrots* (from the French of Jules Reynard) / *The Cherry Orchard / The Married Women / The Great Adventure / The Return of the Prodigal / A Doll's House / The Little Stone House / You Never Can Tell / Trelawney of the Wells*

1912   *Macaire* (played the lead) / *Rutherford and Son* / *Big Hit* / *The Combat*

1913   *Mrs Warren's Profession* / *The Average Man* (Ken wrote it and played lead) / *Bolt* (Glasgow) / *Magic* (written by G K Chesterton especially for Ken and presented at the Lyric Theatre, London) / *Geminae* / *Impulse*

1914   *The Three Wayfarers* / *The Music Cure* / *Rhabah* / *Damaged Goods*, *Account Rendered* and *Dusk* / *Magic* (revival) and *Dusk* / *The Hem of the Flag* / *Three Chapters* (all at Little Theatre)

Writing

'A Suicide that Failed' – short story, 1912

'The Vicar's Mite' – short story, 1912

'The Happiest Time' – short story, 1912; later made into film (about 1919)

Till Our Ship Comes In – novel, 1912; published 1919

The Dead Pierott – poems, 1912; published 1919

The Practical Course in Cinema Acting in Ten Complete Lessons – by Mary Pickford, Charlie Chaplin and others; includes 'The Work of the Film Producer' by Kenelm Foss; 1920

Nuncs' Causeway – novel, 1928

'How I Began' – article, 1928

'A Present From Home' – short story, 1935

'His Own Court Jester' – short story, 1935

The Double Life of J M Turner – biography, 1938; new edition 1951

Here Lies Richard Brinsley Sheridan – biography, 1939; republished 1949

Unwedded Bliss: Sixty examples of famous folk who, eschewing the 'honourable estate' and 'excellent mystery' of matrimony, fulfilled their hearts' desires in diverse ways – 1949

Beardsley: His Best Fifty Drawings – selected by Kenelm Foss, 1949

Bohemian Lovesong – novel, 1950; published 1958

The Wages of Sin – novel, 1950

The Best of A J Alan – selected and introduced by Kenelm Foss, 1954

A Swinburne Anthology – biographical introduction by Kenelm Foss, 1955

Film

In 1917, soon after entering the film world, he formed the company Lucky Cat Films with two actor friends, Guy Newall and George Clark. He worked as a scenario writer and later wrote many films, starring in many as well. He worked with the film mogul W H Thompson for many years.

The Man Without a Soul – based on the story by Kenelm Foss, who also starred, 1916

The Manxman – Adapted from Hall Caine's novel by Kenelm Foss, who also played the part of Ross, 1916

Tinker, Tailor, Soldier, Sailor – written by Kenelm Foss, 1918

The Divine Gift – written by Kenelm Foss, 1918

Peace, Perfect, Peace – written to commemorate the signing of the Armistice by Kenelm Foss, 1918

The Wages of Sin – written by and starring Kenelm Foss, 1918

The Top Dog – thriller adapted from Fergus Hume's novel by Kenelm Foss, 1918

Till Our Ship Comes In – Foss's own novel made into a six-part weekly serial. Written and produced by Kenelm Foss, 1919

Cricket on the Quicksands! – presented by Kenelm Foss, 1919

The Double Life of Mr Alfred Burton – from the novel by Philip Oppenheim; starring and written by Kenelm Foss, 1919

A Little Bit of Fluff – adapted and directed by Kenelm Foss, 1919

I Will – Lucky Cat Films' first production, which received much acclaim; written and directed by Kenelm Foss, 1919

Not Guilty – written by Kenelm Foss, who also played the lead, 1919

The Joyous Adventures of Aristide Pujol – starring (and produced by) Kenelm Foss, 1920

The Breed of the Treshams – from the play by Beulah Marie Dix; written and directed by Kenelm Foss, 1920

The Glad Eye – adapted, designed and produced by Kenelm Foss, 1920

The Street of Adventure – adapted, designed and produced by Kenelm Foss, 1921

The Headmaster – starring Cyril Maude; directed by Kenelm Foss, 1921

All Roads Lead to Calvary – adapted and directed by Kenelm Foss, 1921

No. 5 John Street – from the novel by Richard Whiteing, starring Zenn Dare; written and directed by Kenelm Foss, 1921

Cherry Ripe – directed by Kenelm Foss, 1921

The House of Peril – starring Fay Compton; written and directed by Kenelm Foss, 1922

A Bachelor Husband – by Ruby M Ayres; adapted, designed and produced by Kenelm Foss, 1922

Dicky Monteith – adapted, designed and produced by Kenelm Foss, 1922

The Wonderful Year – from the novel by W J Locke; written and directed by Kenelm Foss, 1922

A Romance of Old Baghdad – adapted and directed by Kenelm Foss, 1922

Kean (Désorde et génie) – adapted from Alexandre Dumas' play by Kenelm Foss, 1924

Henry Ainley was a matinée idol of the early part of the last century. He acted with Ken at the Old Vic and they remained friends all their lives.

Reproduced by kind permission of the Department of Rare Books and Special Collections, University of Rochester Library, New York.

Hillam,
Burnham.
Somerset.

22nd Sept. 1922

My dear Reader Too.,

I didn't think Yes, (F. is!) here when we jointly produced "D. D. Ecclesia" in the Abbey prayer-room (entrance fee: five biscuits) that I should ever do it for a living; but I'm now doing it & I remember as if it were last night, you all ate the biscuits. I am running down here in the country —

married etc. I only came up to Town when I had to. Cyril Maude was talking to me about "You and the Stage" to-night— The *ties 2 uniforms*. He too has I'm told been very ill — and if that is so I hope you are recovering fast — and have you been to my friends & from there Sir Arne (he was running when I saw him) Claying [?] at flying at Station near the Station

Dear Foss, I have been waiting — I will tell Lawrence to send you a copy of my novel "A Cuckoo in the Nest" which has some pretty useful — and you might use the actor to do use the good lines of talking (god knows it wouldn't make a good film) nor be a chance that I should think might be "The Diplomat" too is that direction. Well, it is good to hear from you again — and I hope I may get a chance of seeing you before long. Certainly next time I come to town I will phone + see whether you are there + if so come down + look you up.

I perpetrated "The Diplomat" some time ago and Reandy took it to his cocktail play + arranged to tie presentation of it across of Carlton College, to Reginald took it on for Maude.

With many thanks for writing out — Yours
Ben Travers

Benjamin Travers

When young, Ben Travers and Kenelm Foss were at prep school together but lost touch after a while. They met up years later quite by chance visiting a theatre and stayed friends for ever after.

> Feb 22, 1910
>
> 2½ Shaftesbury Avenue
> W.C.
>
> 22 — 2 — 10
>
> Kenelm Foss
>
> My Dear Foss;
> "Happy indeed would
> be the arts if artists done
> instead of them". I am
> delighted to know that "Columbine"
> pleased you so well. I only
> hope that you will never
> regret your rash promise to
> buy seats for my future efforts.
>
> very sincerely
> Harold Chapin
>
> Harold Chapin

Harold Chapin worked with Ken at the Repertory Theatre in Glasgow.

Reproduced by kind permission of the Department of Rare Books and Special Collections, University of Rochester Library, New York.

Theatre Royal
Nottingham

Dear Kenelm

Very many thanks for your letter & offer which I hope very much we shall be able to pay up. Just at present I am touring with 'The Rainbow' which concludes on April 4th. If necessary however, I think I can get out of the last week & anyway I shouldn't be too far off to come up to rehearsals. We are at the Court Liverpool next week after that we are down at Brighton. Could I see you on the morning of Monday week — the 9th proximo & talk things over — as I could stop up in town on that day. So very glad that Aufric has turned out so successful. Mine is playing with me & has made a great success. You would find her very useful. I'm sure if there is anything doing that might suit her.

Yours sincerely
Roland Pertwee

Ronald Pertwee and Ken were teenage friends acting in many amature plays around Croydon, Surrey, where Kenelm lived at the time.

Reproduced by kind permission of the Department of Rare Books and Special Collections, University of Rochester Library, New York.

July 13, 1939

**STORNOWAY HOUSE,
CLEVELAND ROW,
ST JAMES'S.**

13th July 1939.

Kenelm Foss

Dear Mr. Foss,

Thank you for your letter.

I already have a copy of your book on Sheridan. I have not yet finished it. It is still at my bedside, because my bed is my resting place when I read.

I will write you again later on.

Yours sincerely,

Beaverbrook

William Maxwell Aitken, 1st Baron Beaverbrook

First met in Fleet Street and stayed friends for many a year

Kenelm Foss, Esq.,
24, Russell Road,
Kensington, W.14.

William Maxwell Aitken and Kenelm Foss first met in Fleet Street, London and stayed friends for many a year.

Reproduced by kind permission of the Department of Rare Books and Special Collections, University of Rochester Library, New York.

A.F.35.

Dec 5. 1953

9 Swan Court
Chelsea
S.W.3

5 Dec 1953

Kenelm Foss

My dear Kenelm,
Thanks for your two letters. As I told you I can't do anything on the scheme till after Christmas, and then we'll have to talk.

I'm glad you liked the R+S introduction. I persuaded it in the reference to you was in before you wrote! I didn't hear it myself as I was taking the Chair somewhere that night, and Pettysell an old Rutherford didn't sound attractive.

Yours ever
Sir Lewis T Casson   Lewis Casson

Kenelm Foss and Sir Lewis T Casson met in early theatre days. They shared a flat in Clifford's Inn, London, and became lifelong friends.

Reproduced by kind permission of the Department of Rare Books and Special Collections, University of Rochester Library, New York.

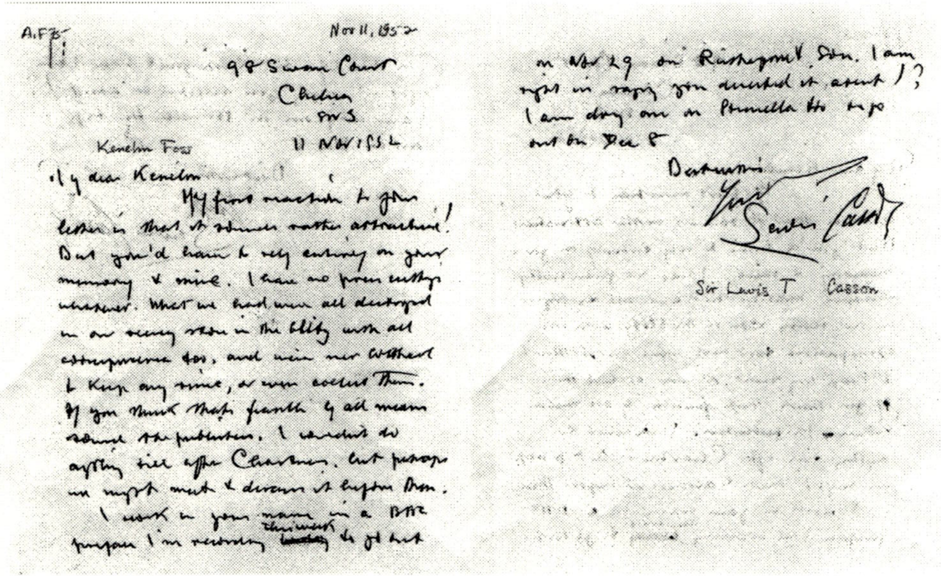

A letter from Ken's lifelong friend, Sir Lewis T Casson.

Reproduced by kind permission of the Department of Rare Books and Special Collections, University of Rochester Library, New York.

This is the first book FANNY BURNEY has written. She was inspired to write about the life of her father, Kenelm Foss, following a challenge from one of her grandchildren. It has taken her exactly three years to gather and put together all the information for this book, which she wrote entirely in longhand. She lives in the attractive village of West End in Esher, Surry, and her hobbies are gardening, sketching and walking.